Soccer Training

08 LO 11

D0416186

Soccer Training

INCLUDES 100 PRACTICE DRILLS

Mervin Beck
Stuart Biddle
Anne de Looy
Peter Thomas

The Crowood Press

First published in 1989 by
The Crowood Press Ltd
Ramsbury, Marlborough
Wiltshire SN8 2HR

New edition 1995
This impression 1999

© The Crowood Press Ltd 1990, except Chapter 3 © Anne de Looy 1989

All rights reserved. No part of this publication may be reproduced or transmitted
in any form or by any means, electronic or mechanical, including photocopy,
recording, or any information storage and retrieval system, without permission in
writing from the publishers.

British Library Cataloguing in Publication Data

A catalogue record for this book is available from the British Library.

ISBN 1-85223-896-8

Acknowledgements
Line Illustrations for Chapter 1 by Vanetta Joffe

Typeset by Acūté, Stroud
Printed by J. W. Arrowsmith, Bristol

Contents

THE AUTHORS

MERVYN BECK: Mervyn is Principal Lecturer in physical education at the Carnegie Department of Leeds Metropolitan University. He has worked in the UK and abroad with the Football Association Coaching scheme and is a fully licensed FA coach. He managed Great Britain's students team from 1970 until 1976 and is involved with coaching children at the coaching centres in Leeds.

Dr STUART BIDDLE: Stuart is a senior lecturer in the School of Education, University of Exeter, where he is the course director of the MSc degree in Exercise and Sport Psychology and president of the European Federation of Sport Psychology. He is an active consultant in sport and exercise and was formerly an international weightlifting competitor and coach.

Dr ANNE DE LOOY: Anne is head of Dietetics and Nutrition at Queen Margaret College, Edinburgh, and tutor to the National Coaching Foundation on sports nutrition.

Dr PETER THOMAS: Peter is a sports physician in Reading and was an Olympic oarsman in the Mexico Games of 1968. He was then the Great Britain rowing team doctor and is currently the medical director of Reading Sports Injury Clinic and a medical officer at the British Olympic Association's Medical Centre at Northwick Park.

Introduction

Soccer is one of the most popular team games in the world and it remains at the forefront of sporting interest and popularity in Britain. You only need to see the extensive coverage given to the sport in the media to realise its huge following.

However, people play sport for a variety of reasons, ranging from having fun, to health and fitness, competition, making friends, skill development and others. Whatever the main reason might be for playing soccer, it is likely that most players wish to improve or maintain their playing skills, including physical fitness. This involves preparing well for matches so that enjoyment is maximised.

Today in soccer, as in most sports, success is usually only achieved through a well-planned and executed training programme. The purpose of this book, therefore, is to outline some of the fundamentals of such a training programme from which players of all levels will benefit. However, whereas most sports books – for reasons of space – concentrate on the technical and tactical skills of the game, this book aims to provide a more complete picture of the training process by looking at:

(i)   soccer practices;
(ii)   physical fitness;
(iii)   nutrition;
(iv)   injury prevention;
(v)   mental training.

This all-round approach is recommended as the best way of preparing yourself for the game of soccer.

1 Individual and Group Practices

Soccer is a team game, but the standard of play which is achieved will always depend upon the level of proficiency of each player. Players are often described as being particularly skilful and this chapter looks at ways in which an individual's skills can be improved. There are many definitions of skill but for the purposes of this book it may be defined as the ability to utilise the appropriate technique at the correct time, having made a good decision, as a result of the information presented to the player by the game. Skill therefore has several components which can be represented as shown in Diagram A. Fitness and mental approach are dealt with in Chapters 2 and 5 and so this chapter will concentrate on technique and decision-making.

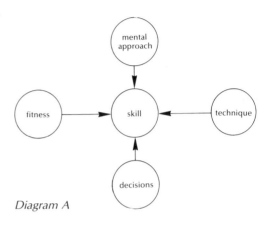

Diagram A

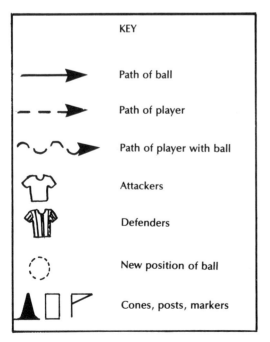

In the game of soccer there are three elements which interact with each other; space, time and pressure. Whenever you carry out any technique, you will have varying amounts of space and time and be under more or less pressure from opponents. In the learning and practice situation you can control the factor of pressure and use as much space and time as is needed in order to improve technique. When you later apply techniques to the game or to practices, this is known as skill.

It is firmly believed that British players do not practise technique enough, so this chapter concentrates upon technique and develops your skill using progressive practices. In order to improve technique you should practise both on your own and with others. Eventually, after hundreds and thousands of touches of the ball your feet become accustomed to the ball and you develop the ability and confidence to carry out all the game techniques with poise, relaxation and balance. To begin with we shall consider what can be done on your own and using a ball.

INDIVIDUAL PRACTICES

For all the drills in this section (Nos 1 – 15) the requirements are basic – you need nothing more than a flat piece of ground and a football.

Running with the Ball

(1)   Stroke the ball in turn with the inside and then the outside of your foot, making sure that you also use your weak (non-preferred) foot. Keep your head up and concentrate on what would be going on around you if you were playing in a game, using your peripheral vision to allow you to control the ball. When running fast the ball should be pushed well in front of your feet to allow optimum speed. However, when moving slowly you should keep the ball close to your feet to maximise control. Practise changes in both speed and direction and then incorporate a spinning turn – in which you pivot around the ball, keeping your foot on it as you do so.

Dribbling Practices

These practices are designed to enable you to go past opposing players while still remaining in possession of the ball. This is a valuable skill of particular use for attacking players.

(2)   Running quickly with the ball, with your head up and using your arms for balance, feint to the left with your body but accelerate away to the right with the ball. This can be repeated in the other direction by feinting to the right with your body. An alternative feinting action is to pass your right foot over the ball, as if you were going to take it to the right but instead accelerating away to the left. This

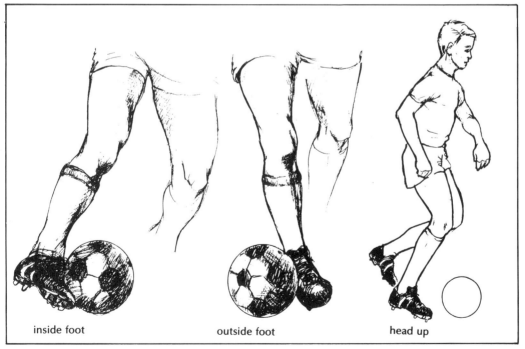

inside foot   outside foot   head up

Drill 1

feint can also be done if you step over the ball with your left foot and then accelerate away to the right. You can also pretend to stop and then accelerate away in the same direction in order to overtake an opponent.

(3) Repeat Drill 2 using a skittle or post as an imaginary defender so that you can practise the timing of your point of acceleration.

Drill 3

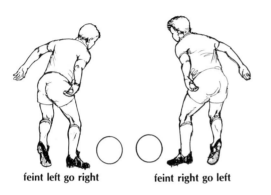

feint left go right   feint right go left

Drill 2

Coaching Points

Only look down at the ball when you are about to change direction and need to control the ball closely. Try to relax your body as much as you can. Moving, feinting, accelerating, stopping and restarting are all parts of dribbling technique which you can practise alone. Practise any techniques of dribbling which you may see on television, such as the 'Cruyff turn', the 'Beardsley hip wiggle' or the 'Barnes screen and accelerate away'.

One-bounce and One-touch Routines

(4)   Make the ball bounce about two feet off the ground and practise kicking it gently into the air; never let the ball bounce more than once before you kick it into the air again. Stay light and bouncy on your feet and begin to touch it alternately with each foot. Then kick

cover the ball
left or right

Drill 2

THE HENLEY COLLEGE LIBRARY

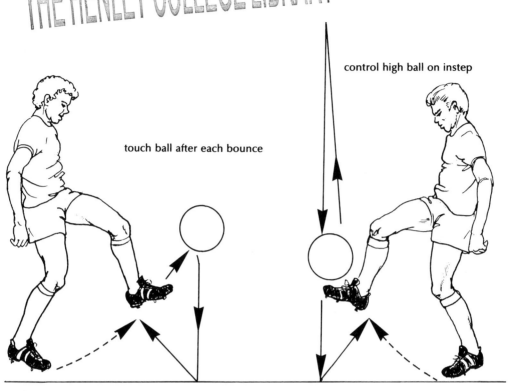

control high ball on instep

touch ball after each bounce

Drill 4

the ball high above your head, controlling it on your instep and letting it drop to the ground before continuing a low-bounce rhythm. Practise mixing the high kick and control with the low-bounce routine.

(5) Keep the ball off the ground by kicking it with one foot, whilst bouncing up and down on the other – keep the ball about six inches above the kicking foot. Try to manage this for thirty seconds before changing to your other foot for another thirty seconds. Then try four touches on one foot followed by four touches on the other foot. Do this drill for thirty seconds or longer if possible. This practice helps you to both strengthen the ankle and develop good ball touch.

(6) Practise one touch from your foot to your knee, your head, your shoulder, your chest, your thigh and so on. See how many consecutive touches you can make. Remember to

keep the ball
off the ground

Drill 5

11

bounce lightly on your feet to maintain a good balance and to keep the body prepared for a movement in any direction. Try to beat your highest score.

(7)   Combine the ball-bounce of Drill 4 and the ball-touch of Drill 5 with a sudden movement away from the spot, running with the ball as you do so. Repeat this in the sequence: ball-touch – move from the spot – stop – lift the ball – bounce the ball and control it — etc.

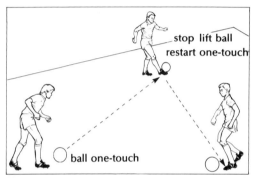

Drill 7

Coaching Points

Always remember the importance of good footwork. You need to be as agile as a dancer or a boxer; very light on your feet, bouncy and ready to move in any direction. Do not hit the ball too hard but coax the ball into the air or along the ground and work at as many consecutive touches as possible. Once you can regularly get beyond thirty touches you are well under way.

Using a Wall

A wall can be very useful when practising ball skills. If the surface is uneven it gives a random nature to the return of the ball and therefore keeps you alert. Here are some practices which will sharpen your technique – depending, of course, upon how close you are to the wall and how hard you kick the ball.

(8)   Kick the ball on to the wall and receive the rebound, controlling it with one touch. Then hit the wall again. Work on stabilising the ball with one touch and if it is too close to your feet after the touch, move away from the ball in order to make space for your next kick.

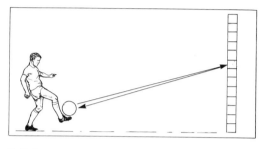

Drill 8

(9)   Make a target on the wall as shown. After controlling the ball with one touch from the rebound, hit the target area only.

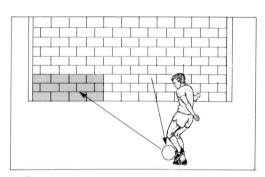

Drill 9

(10)   Give yourself low and high targets as shown, this will mean you can make some returns that are chipped or lobbed.

(11)   Meet the ball on the rebound; turn, controlling the ball with one touch to the left or right. Move round a positioned marker dribbling the ball. Shoot at the wall again.

(12)   Practise a one-bounce routine against the wall using alternate feet. Concentrate on your footwork in particular.

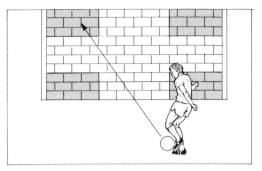

Drill 10

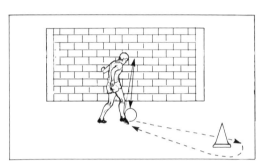

Drill 11

Drill 12

Drill 13

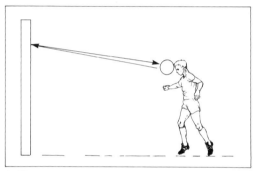

Drill 14

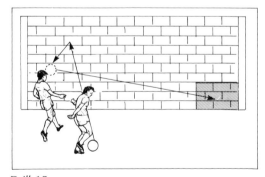

Drill 15

(13)   Practise volleying against the wall using either foot and see how many volley-touch returns you can make. Twelve would be very good but make sure your footwork is always neat.

(14)   Practise heading volleys against the wall. Try to achieve as many consecutive headers as you can.

(15)   Develop your heading technique by jumping for the return. Then practise aiming at a set target area. Work for power and accuracy, whether you are an attacker or a defender, as you will need both skills in a

Drill 15

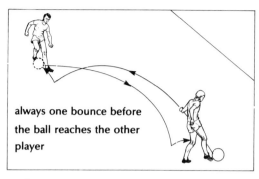

always one bounce before the ball reaches the other player

Drill 16

game. Remember to draw your head and neck back as you jump and then thrust the head towards the ball with your neck muscles. Look through the ball to the target and hit the ball with the forehead; no other part of the head should be used.

PRACTISING WITH A FRIEND

Many of the practices which were suggested for a single player will be appropriate for practise in pairs. So in this section you will need to add a partner and some cones to your practice sessions.

A Ball and a Friend

(16)   Decide on an area in which you will try to keep the ball, say ten metres square. Keep the ball moving between you and your partner in this area; allow only one bounce before your partner touches the ball. Be aware of using good footwork. Your partner should be made to move but allowed a chance to get to the ball, you are not competing yet.

(17)   Practise keeping the ball off the ground; touch it four times and then pass.

(18)   Following on from Drill 17, progress to two touches and then pass to your partner.

(19)   Progress to alternate touches for each player.

(20)   Practise running, dodging and turning with the ball. Your partner should stay as close as possible behind you.

simply preventing the other player reaching the ball (shadowing)

Drill 20

(21)   For this drill start off side by side on line XY and roll the ball away. One player should say 'go' and then both sprint to the ball. The first person to take possession should keep it from the other player for as long as possible.

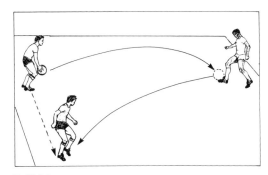

Drill 23

(24)   Progress to moving backwards and forwards snaking across the width of the pitch area.

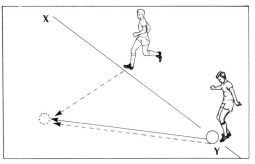

Drill 21

(22)   Begin by standing five yards apart. Throw the ball randomly to your partner who must return it to you with one touch only, from either the left or right foot, thigh or knee, head, chest or any part of the body. Your partner must be running on the spot all the time and the drill is best continued for alternate one-minute sessions.

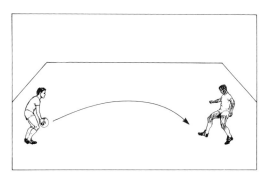

Drill 22

(23)   Repeat Drill 22, but serve and then move to a new spot. Your partner must get the ball to you with one touch from any part of the body.

Drill 25

15

(25) Whilst standing ten metres apart in an area of twenty metres by ten metres pass the ball to your partner. As soon as your partner touches the ball you may move forwards. Your partner has to dribble the ball past you to reach the end-line you are defending. You must therefore prevent him or her from doing this, paying particular attention to avoiding any physical contact.

(26) **Thread passes.** Begin with A on the end-line and B ten metres in front on the pitch. A passes the ball to B and then sprints beyond B to position A1. Player B turns and plays the ball into A's path so A will meet it at position A1. Repeat this action across the pitch with B running to position B1 and so on.

(27) **Long and short passes.** With A and B positioned thirty or forty metres apart, A lofts a pass to B and runs towards B's position. B gives a first-time return pass to A at A1 who then returns the ball to B. B now dribbles the ball to where A started and repeats the routine.

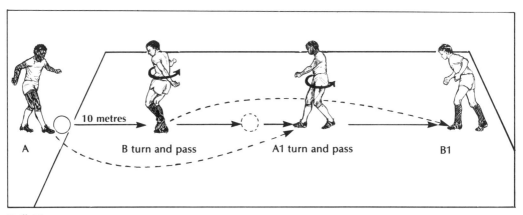

Drill 26

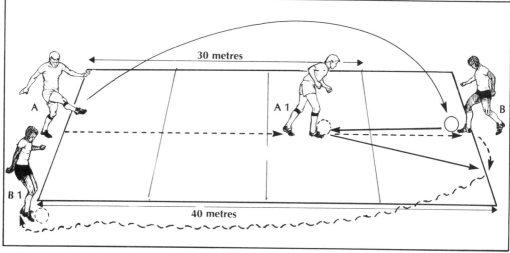

Drill 27

Using a Wall

(28) Practise alternate passes on to the wall. Make sure that you use only one touch for control and one touch for the pass back on to the wall.

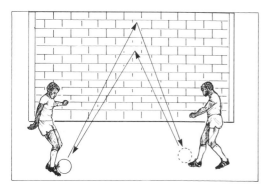

Drill 28

(29) Using a variation on the one-bounce routine you practised in Drill 12; the ball must now bounce in a certain space as it rebounds off the wall to your partner. A marker line of five metres from the wall is a useful boundary to start with, progressing to ten yards as you continue alternate touches between your partner and yourself.

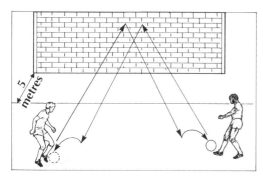

Drill 29

(30) Try volley touches against the wall between your partner and yourself, keeping the ball off the ground all the time.

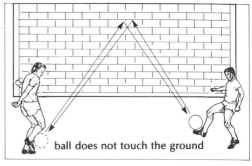

ball does not touch the ground

Drill 30

(31) Vary your practice hits on to the wall by meeting your own rebound and, under control, turning with the ball. As you turn, pass the ball to your partner who must then repeat the exercise.

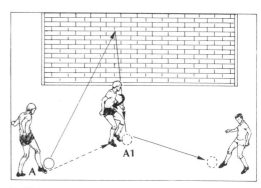

Drill 31

(32) **Wall game.** Mark out a space twenty metres by ten metres in front of the wall. Practise the one-bounce routine of Drill 29, but make the ball bounce in to your partner's marked standing area (ABCD). Vary the practice by letting it bounce in either your or your partner's standing area but not nearer than five metres from the wall.

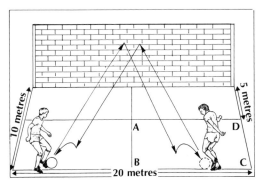

Drill 32

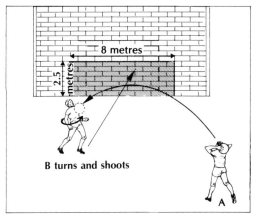

B turns and shoots

(33)   Using a goal area marked out on the wall of height two-and-a-half metres and width eight metres, A passes to B on the pitch. B then attempts to dribble past A, who is positioned between B and the goal, in order to shoot at the goal. Alternate playing positions.

Drill 34

(35)   **Six-shot competition.** Whilst defending the target goal A should pass the ball forwards to B who should be twenty metres away when receiving the ball and then B shoots at the goal. A trys to stop B scoring and may use hand contact if required. The aim is to see how many goals, in six attempts, each player can achieve.

Drill 33

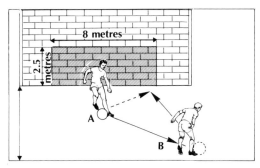

Drill 35

(34)   A begins by throwing the ball to B as if taking a throw-in. B must control the ball on his or her chest, thigh or instep, then turn to shoot at the goal. A should practise serving from different angles and A and B should alternate positions.

(36)   A centres the ball, with a kick or a throw, to B. B then volleys or heads the ball at the goal area. Practise this drill six times each.
(37)   **Penalty competition.** Begin with A in goal so that B has the first twelve shots from the penalty spot. When A has completed his

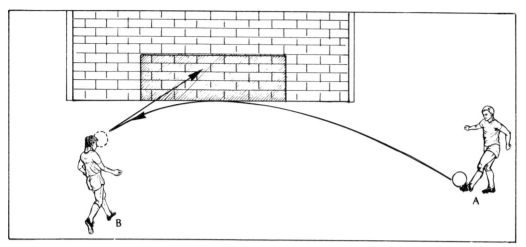

Drill 36

or her twelve attempts the number of goals scored can be compared to see which player is the best.

GROUP PRACTICES

By adding a number of players to the drills you will ensure continued improvement in technique and fitness for speed or stamina depending upon the way in which the practices are conducted.

Practising with Three Players

In addition to practices involving two against one, the coaching unit of three allows easy organisation and continuity. As there are now three players the next section of drills are based on a simple routine of A passing to B and then following the ball, B passing to C and then following the ball and finally C passing to A and then following the ball.

(38) Following the organisation shown in the illustration, each player should dribble the ball across the space, feint to the left or right and then pass the ball to the next player.

(39) Moving across the space again progress to spinning on the ball in the middle through 360 degrees and then passing the ball to the next player.

(40) Vary the practice by moving across the space while keeping the ball off the ground. Try to pass to the next player keeping the ball in the air and see if all three of you can keep the ball off the ground for as long as possible. Use your feet, thighs, chest, head or shoulders.

(41) Throw or kick (chip) the ball across the space. You must control the ball with your chest, thigh or foot before passing it again across the space. Always follow your throw or pass to keep the organisation going.

(42) **Long and short passes.** A passes the ball across the space and follows the pass. He or she receives a return pass and then plays a short pass to B. This is now repeated to C.

(43) Follow Drill 42 but chip or loft the ball to the next player. From now on ensure that all touches of the ball are one touch only.

(44) A throws the ball across the space to B and follows the throw. B heads to C and follows the ball. C serves to A and follows the ball, while A heads to B and so on. When serving make the player jump as high as possible to head the ball.

19

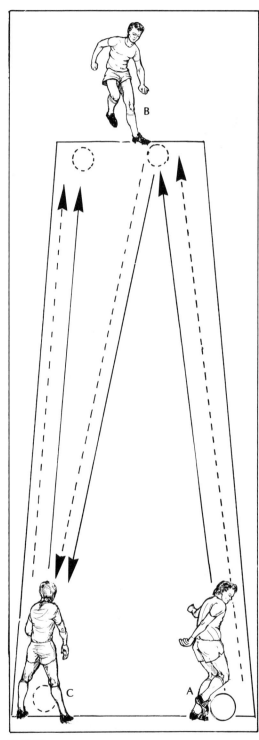

Drill 38

(45)   Continue to follow the set organisation, but this time begin by chipping the ball over, or bending the ball round the oncoming player. Remember to follow the pass.

(46)   **One-bounce routine.** Using the basic organisation progress to lobbing the ball over the advancing player so that the ball bounces before reaching the next player.

(47)   **Continuous heading.** Using an area of five metres try to keep the ball in the air. Head the ball from A to B to C and after heading it remember to move quickly across the space. Try to keep the ball in the air for at least twenty continuous touches.

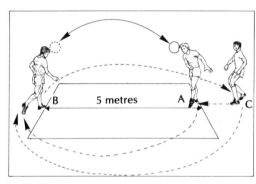

Drill 47

For Drills 48–50 the only requirement is an area to play in of roughly forty metres square.

(48)   **Random volley touch.** Begin with player A throwing the ball to either of the other players. The player receiving the pass must return the ball with a one-touch volley to either of the other two players, using the head, thigh or foot.

(49)   Practise Drill 48 but begin to move quickly round the pitch area. Serve the ball high enough to give the other players time to move to it and try not to make it too easy. Move to new places so that the next player to pass has to adjust in order to aim at a new target. If the ball is in the air for two seconds, the other players should be able to run at least

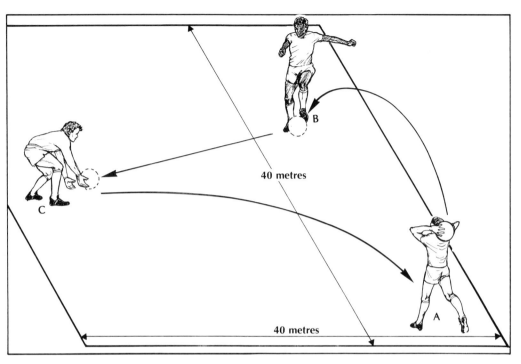

40 metres

40 metres

Drill 48

ten metres. Repeat with one touch to control and one touch for a ground pass to either player.

(50) Progress from Drills 48 and 49 to random services to either player and quick movements to new spaces. The ball must be returned with one touch from either the head, a volley using the inside of the foot or a volley using the thigh or knee. Make sure that the services are good enough to achieve these practices.

Practising with Four Players

Obviously the practices given for pairs and threes can also be used for four players, but when it comes to competition with two against two, practice becomes very energetic and considerably more tiring. The next section of practice drills requires a playing area of roughly forty metres square, four players and two coloured bibs.

(51) **Random volleys.** Begin the drill with A serving to B and with C and D defending. B must return the ball to A with a volley; A will need to move very quickly into space. In order for every player to practise the individual techniques involved you will need to rotate the serving and volleying partners A and B; as well as eventually switching the defending partners (C and D) into the role of A and B.

(52) **Throw-in and pass.** A throws to B, C and D defend. C is just outside the playing area until B touches the ball. A and B must try to make three or four passes before C and D touch the ball. B must return the ball to A with one touch and A should try to give a good throw by 'floating' the ball to B. If the pressure on B is too much, practise with D at various positions but starting ten metres away until B has touched the ball. The first partnership should have six attempts before C and D have the opening throw-in.

Drill 51

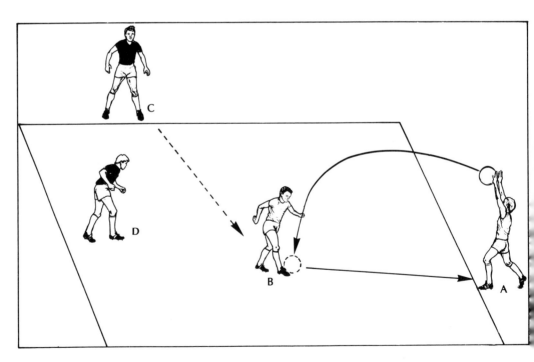

Drill 52

(53)   **Throw-in and screen (shield) the ball.** Practise Drill 52 but now B must control the ball and screen it until A takes up a new position. C and D are allowed to move as soon as B touches the ball. Try to make three or four passes between pairs, but screen the ball from your opponents until your partner can get into a position to receive the pass.

Drill 53

Coaching Point

Position yourself between the defender and the ball in a sideways-on attitude, leaning slightly towards the defender.

Practising with Five Players

Again, all the practices described for threes can be used in a group of five players.

(54)   The basic organisation is for A, C and E to stand in a line fifteen metres from B and D. To begin A passes the ball to B and follows the ball across to join the queue behind D. Then B passes the ball to C and follows the ball to join the queue behind E. Depending on the distance between A and B and the speed with which the players move across the space, this drill improves technique, speed and stamina, in any combination, over a period of time.

For the next two drills you require a playing area of thirty metres square and five players.

(55)   **Consecutive passes.** A, B and C must try to make as many passes as possible before D and E touch the ball. Change the players around so each practises within a two and a three.
(56)   **Conditioning the practice.** Repeat Drill 55 with the following variation of either a two-touch play or no running with the ball.

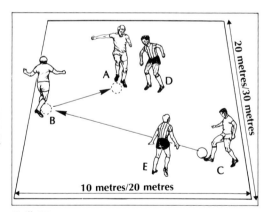

Drill 55

Coaching Points (Diagrams B–D)

Encourage your team-mates to move. Pass softly to a space for them to move towards the ball (Diagram B). Pass firmly to their feet if you

Diagram B

want to play a wall pass (Diagrams C and D) and receive the ball back again. It is important to talk to each other using phrases such as 'hold it', 'man on', 'play feet' and so on. Give good positive information to each other. Be confident and try not to give the ball away.

Practices for Defenders

The following drills require an area to play in of ten metres square with two players only.

(57) **Jockeying.** This is the technique involved in delaying an opponent and is a very important aspect of the skill of defending. A passes to B, as soon as B touches the ball A must close him or her down and practise jockeying him or her back to line XY. Swap roles so that player B, who passes to A, jockeys him or her back to line PQ.

(58) As for Drill 57 except A passes to B and then immediately closes in on B in order to reduce the space between them. This movement time is important for the defender, since it is advantageous to delay the attacker as soon as possible.

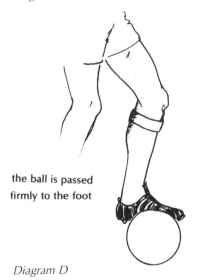

Diagram C

the ball is passed firmly to the foot

Diagram D

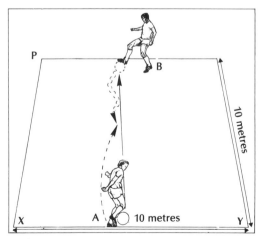

Drill 57

Coaching Points (Diagram E)

Players should practise jockeying with a side-ways stance, moving as quickly as possible backwards and keeping their feet shoulder-width apart. Both feet should be moved at the same time (like a boxer) and should not come together in a side-skip action nor should they become too far apart. The body should be balanced and ready to move in any direction if the feet are kept shoulder-width apart.

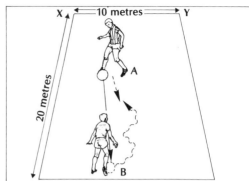

Drill 59

Diagram E

(59) Practise this drill, which is similar to Drill 57, but play over a distance of twenty metres. A passes to B and immediately goes to delay B's progress. B tries to dribble past A to line XY.

Coaching Points (Diagrams F and G)

Defending angle of approach. Diagram F shows right back defender B approaching the left winger A in such a way as to invite A to go down the wing. This is a good general ploy since this is the longest way to the goal, although it may not always be the correct decision if the winger is fast and good at crossing. If this is the case, then it may be better to bring the winger inside (*see* Diagram G). If you do bring a player inside, you will need to know that you are covered and generally the player C behind you should help by saying 'bring him inside' or 'keep him down the line'. Tactics such as these should be pre-planned, especially when you know you are up against a fast or tricky winger. Remember that if you bring a player inside, you may leave yourself vulnerable to a shot at goal.

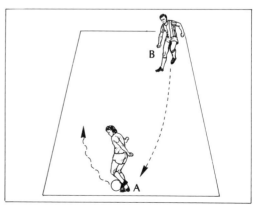

Diagram F

Diagram G

Many wing forwards favour one foot for control and ball-touch and whenever this is the case it is often sound strategy to force the player on to the other foot. Again, this will often be pre-planned but an intelligent defender should always be able to see where this is the case and so take any necessary action.

Generally speaking, therefore, a defender will make the attacker go the long way round (force him or her down the wing) unless he or she gets an instruction from defenders behind, who are covering, to do otherwise. This will give the defender's colleagues time to prepare for the cross which may soon follow.

These aspects are part of the preparation for the game, where the strengths and weaknesses of the opponents are discussed and the pre-planned tactics and strategies are decided.

Movement time and decision time. Many young players do not react to a pass

until their opponent is in possession of the ball. This can be costly if the attacker is good at dribbling or running with the ball. Defenders do not like to have attackers running straight at them with the ball and so the sooner they can apply pressure to their opponents, the better will be the defenders' chance of delaying them.

When defending, players should continually be asking themselves whether or not they can get to their opponents if they receive the ball now. This mental attitude should be present every second of the match when a player is defending. This should keep defenders within the correct distance of their opponents and as soon as it is obvious that a pass is going to an attacker, the defenders should move quickly towards this player and reduce the space between themselves and the attacker. As the player arrives a decision has to be made such as 'can I intercept the pass?', 'shall I delay the player?', 'shall I tackle the player?', 'which way shall I delay (inside or outside)?', 'can I put him or her under pressure just as he or she touches the ball and if his or her control is not good, can I steal the ball?' It can be appreciated that this is a tall order for a defender, especially while marking a tricky player but the general principles should be:

(i)   move towards the player as the ball is travelling to him or her;
(ii)   stop the attacker turning towards your own goal;
(iii)   stop the attacker shooting at your own goal;
(iv)   stop the attacker running at you with the ball;
(v)   stop the attacker crossing the ball.

If you cannot intercept the pass be patient and delay the player; you may be able to tackle or steal the ball later. Remember that the longer you can delay an attacker the more time your team-mates will have to recover and defend, so forming cover behind you. A good maxim is; 'stay on your feet and do not tackle unless you know you can win that ball'.

Defending by heading. When defenders head the ball they generally try to head for distance or height – or both – they want to clear the ball from the danger zone (especially the penalty area) and the further the ball goes the better. Failing this, if you head the ball high, you will at least gain time to return your body and your feet to a stable position so that you can jump and attack the ball when it comes down again. You may also win time for your goalkeeper to be able to move, jump and catch the ball.

(60) Over the same distance, of twenty metres, as Drill 59; B serves to A so that A can practise heading the ball. A should head the ball over the top of B in order to see how far A can drive B backwards. Switch positions so both of you can practise heading skills.

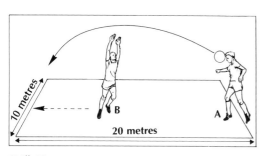

Drill 60

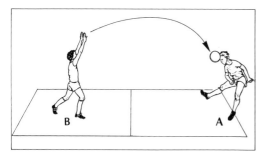

Drill 61

(61) Continue to practise Drill 60 but now as B serves to A, B must throw high into space. A is forced to run and jump to head the ball whilst in the air. Ensure that each player practises this heading technique.

Coaching Points

When heading a ball from a stationary position, the power comes from the legs, back and neck, as you rock back and uncoil the power into the ball. Remember to look through the ball and head only on the forehead (*see* Drill 15).

When practising Drill 61 try to be sideways-on to the ball as it comes towards you. As you jump, bring your neck back and prepare ('cock') your neck muscles. As you arrive at the ball, thrust your head forward with your neck muscles and 'punch' the ball with your forehead. Look through the ball at the angle you wish it to travel.

This practice is difficult and is essentially designed to improve your timing. You need to hit the ball at the top of your jump, so that the power generated from the jump is combined with the thrust of the neck muscles. It is frustrating if you are on your way down when you make contact with the ball as the power from thrusting off the ground is lost – you only have the thrust from your neck muscles. This, however, in some players is considerable. The timing of a jump has to be practised many hundreds of times before a player can combine ground thrust with neck power in order to give that impressive final combination of forces.

Practices for Attackers

When controlling the ball in soccer, the first touch is of great importance – and this is never more apparent than in the skills of an attacker.

THE HENLEY COLLEGE LIBRARY

Coaching Points (Diagrams H–L)

Generally speaking, an attacker quickly comes under pressure from opponents and therefore it is vital that the first touch gives the attacker sufficient space and time to carry out the move decisively.

The first touch made may be any of the following moves: pass first time, shoot or head for the goal first time, control and pass, control and dribble, control and screen (shield) the ball, dribble the ball. It is very important, therefore, in working with young and developing players, that they are encouraged to make decisions as early as possible.

Decision-making. Some of the decisions made will, of course, be wrong but this is less important than actually determining why it was a bad decision. The coach should attempt to correct it with the player during a practice session. It is only after making thousands of decisions and thousands of touches of the ball that a young player can be helped towards making more and more decisions which are 'good'.

I personally believe that young players should be encouraged to think of the decisions they are making as soon as possible. So often the techniques of passing, controlling, shooting and heading are taught, but without combining the process of decision-making. Youngsters are often taught to control the ball, then lift their head, look for the possibilities and then make their decisions. However, I believe that young players should aim to make their decision before the ball arrives. For example, players need to be made aware of the space around them and from where the pressure is coming. Then, before the ball arrives, they can decide which way to move or in which space they should control the ball.

As the game unfolds, a player must continually update his or her decision-making system by asking: 'if the ball came to me now, which space would I go for?', 'where would pressure come from?', 'where would I play my first touch?' By continually rehearsing these mental questions during the game, the player is kept aware of the constantly changing events of the game. It helps with total concentration and is a vital part of good decision-making. Also as a game concept it should be introduced to young players as soon as possible.

Naturally it depends upon the position of the player on the pitch and the severity of the pressure, but even in a crowded penalty area, a forward can keep asking 'can I shoot first time?' and so prepare for the eventuality. In this situation it can often be seen how the first touch robs a forward of an attempt at goal if the decision is to control the ball before shooting. In Diagram H attacker A should aim to control the ball in space X. A should not proceed towards space Y unless he or she decides to dribble past B immediately.

Players should therefore be encouraged to view space and time in terms which directly concern them and continually to update themselves regarding these factors throughout the game. This aspect of their play, called 'spatial awareness', will become second nature as they gain experience. They should be encouraged to view the game plan as shown in Diagram I, so that from A's point of view, he

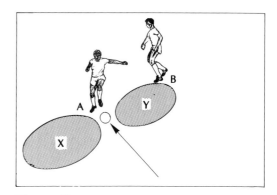

Diagram H

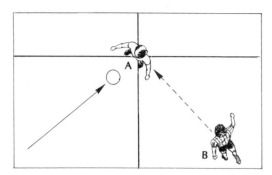

Diagram I

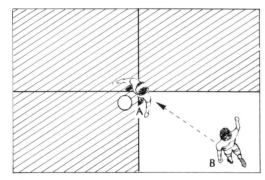

Diagram J

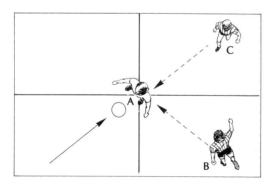

Diagram K

nent is approaching from position B. The space available is therefore all the shaded area. If the picture presented is as shown in Diagram K, then the space available is the area shaded in Diagram L.

Early decision-making eventually gives players precious fractions of a second in which to be slightly ahead of their opponents. If this capacity in young players is not developed, you run the risk that they will have only pre-programmed responses to certain game cues and this will lead to the 'clockwork-player approach'. When given a good background in technique, a player progresses by making increasing numbers of good decisions which are appropriate to the problems set by the game at that particular moment.

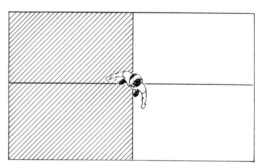

Diagram L

For the following drills you require three players in an area of twenty metres by ten metres.

(62) **Meeting the ball.** Due to the pressure within the game of soccer, a player is often required to sprint forward to meet a pass from a team-mate. This practice should begin with A moving the ball a short distance to signal that the ball is in play, C is a defender. A then passes the ball to B who has to meet the ball. A and B must make three passes without C touching the ball. If C exerts too much pressure on B this can be reduced by placing C five to

or she will have two or more components to consider in making a decision; the approach line of the ball and the approach line of the opponent. It is clear that player A cannot use the space unshaded in Diagram J if the oppo-

29

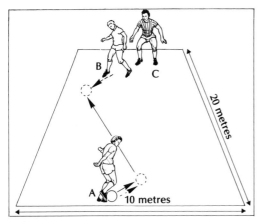

Drill 62

ball away, but after screening for a few seconds A and B should try to make six passes without C touching the ball, each screening it in turn.

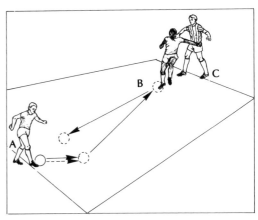

Drill 64

ten paces beyond B, so giving B enough space and time to reach the ball first and make a good pass. Pressure is increased as B progresses.
(63)   Proceed as for Drill 62 but play in an area twenty metres square. A passes to B once the ball is in play and B tries to turn with the ball and beat C to the line XY. If B cannot beat C, then A and B must interpass to get to the line XY.

(65)   For this drill you require an additional player to form two opposing pairs. A serves to B; C and D do not move until B touches the ball. A and B now make as many passes as possible while C and D try to intercept; when they have done so they then make as many passes as possible between themselves. Each player screens the ball whilst waiting for support.

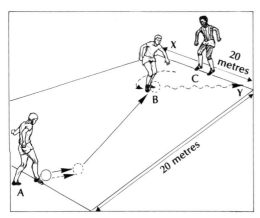

Drill 63

(64)   Continue play as for Drill 63; A again passes to B who has to control the ball and screen (shield) the ball from C for a few seconds. C still tries to intercept or prod the

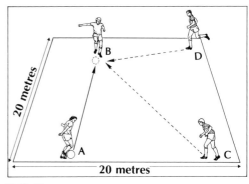

Drill 65

Coaching Points

Moving with the ball. All players should be able to move freely and at speed with the ball, whatever their playing position; practices should therefore include changes of speed and direction. Unlike dribbling, where a player sets out to beat an opponent, running with the ball means keeping the ball away from your feet whilst you run. Accordingly the decision that needs to be made is how often you need to touch the ball; you will therefore need to gauge how near an opponent is, since this will govern how far ahead you can push the ball (and so how often you need to touch it).

Drills 66 and 67 require a group of players in an area forty metres square and for each player to have a ball.

(66) Challenges offered as players move around. Move freely around the space until you hear the command to stop, when you should put your foot on the ball. Move towards the spaces as they develop, pushing the ball into these spaces and then accelerating into them. As you near another player, move into the space between him or her and your ball and move away. Remember not to bump into other players by keeping your head up in order to see their movements. See the ball out of the lower (peripheral) part of your vision and practise turning left and right. Use the inside, outside and the sole of your foot to propel the ball. You should turn quickly, pivoting with your foot on the ball.

(67) Continue Drill 66 but send in a player to steal a ball from any other player – at random. Players should practise shielding the ball or running away into spaces to keep away from the attacking player ('thief').

(68) You will need two players in a channel measuring thirty metres by ten. A runs towards B with the ball and should make sure he or she

Drill 66

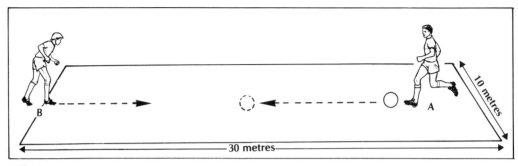

Drill 68

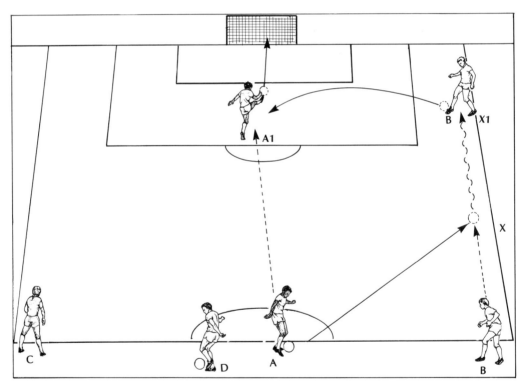

Drill 69

is in control of the ball. A should attempt to make as few touches of the ball as possible before meeting B. A should ensure he or she retains possession. B is free to move when A starts.

(69) All players should work in pairs for this drill in one half of the pitch. They need to work down the left or the right flank with one ball between two players. A plays the ball to the space in front of B at X and runs straight

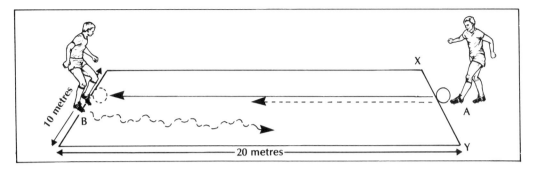

Drill 70

down the field. Sprinting on to the ball B pushes it well ahead and accelerates. At point X1, B crosses the ball and A volley-touches it into the goal. A goalkeeper can be included but is not essential. The exercise is designed to improve your running and crossing skills. As soon as A and B set off, the next pair (C and D) can go. Place any spare players behind the goal to retrieve the balls. After ten runs and centres for each player change positions.

(70) **Dribbling.** This involves trying to beat an opponent while moving with the ball. There are several means of achieving this, two of which are particularly useful; speed and trickery with your feet or body (which temporarily wrong-foots your opponent). To practise dribbling you require two players in a space measuring twenty metres by ten. A plays the ball to B and when B touches it A moves to intercept. To reach line XY B must dribble past A. Take it in turn to dribble the length of the playing area in this way.

Coaching Points

Young players should be encouraged to beat opponents in the attacking half (or final third) of the field and should not be put off by failure. It is important to persuade players to adopt a positive attitude towards beating defenders and they should continually tell themselves that they will be able to go past the opponent. If the defender is good, he or she may win more of the duels, but do not be daunted by the occasional setback. You must believe in your own ability and keep trying and practising.

Drills 71 and 72 require four players training in an area of forty metres by ten.

(71) Player A starts off behind line QR and tries to dribble to the line YZ. Defenders B, C and D try to defend lines ST, UV and WX respectively, without entering the spaces in front of their line. This is difficult for the defenders but it makes it easier for the attacker.
(72) Repeat Drill 71 but all defenders are allowed to move within the grid in front of their line as the attacker enters each grid.
(73) Increase the number of players to between six and twelve and practise in an area of forty by twenty metres. Player A sets off from behind line QR and tries to get to line YZ. Defenders on ST, UV and WX may only move within the grids in front of them and they must not move until A enters their grid. Defenders outside the grids cannot enter but can reach in and intercept the ball if player A gets near to the lines QY or RZ. Points can be awarded as follows: two points for getting into the second grid, five points for reaching the third grid and ten points for moving into the fourth grid.

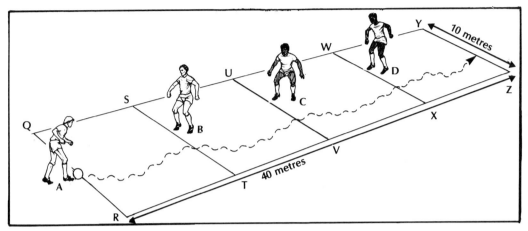

Drill 71

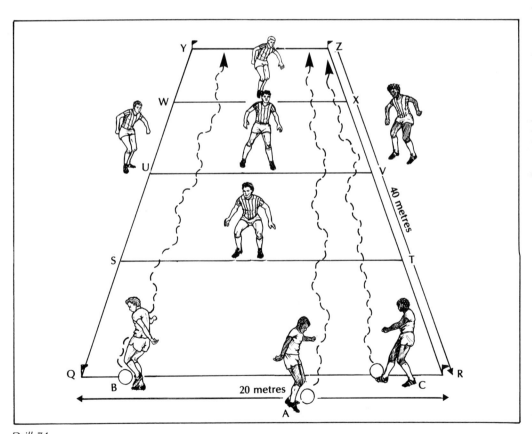

Drill 74

74) A variation on Drill 73 is to let two or three players start off at the same time as A so that at least someone manages to reach the third or fourth grids and scores some points.

To practise Drills 75–80 you require five players and one goal placed centrally in an area of thirty-six metres by forty-four. All play takes place in the two penalty areas on either side of the goal.

75) **Shooting.** A or B shoots from line XY. If the goalkeeper saves the ball he throws it to C or D. They should either shoot first time or pass the ball to their partner. On receiving the pass, either C or D must shoot first time. The ball therefore always passes to the other side of the goal; either after a goal is scored, or from the goalkeeper's throw if the ball is saved. Remember the receivers must either shoot first time or pass to their partner to shoot first time.

(76) Practise Drill 75 but serve the ball in the air from each side. As A throws the ball to B, B can practise either right- or left-footed volleys.

(77) Continue shooting practice as begun in Drill 75 but now progress to serving to your partner from the left or right side. As A serves to B, B can practise shooting, with either the right or left foot, while turning.

(78) This time the pairs (A, B and C, D) take it in turn to practise free kicks (direct and indirect) from just outside the penalty area.

(79) A final variation of Drill 75 begins with A serving the ball to B, whose back is towards the central goal. B should practise turning the ball with one touch and shooting for the goal with the next touch.

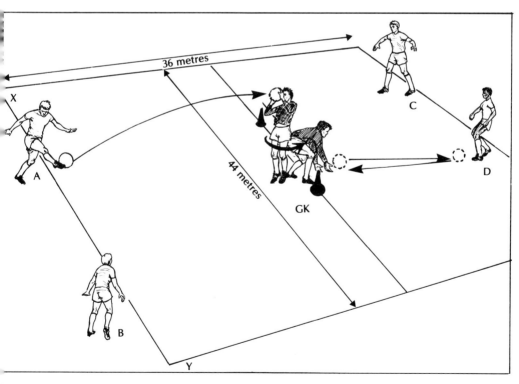

Drill 75

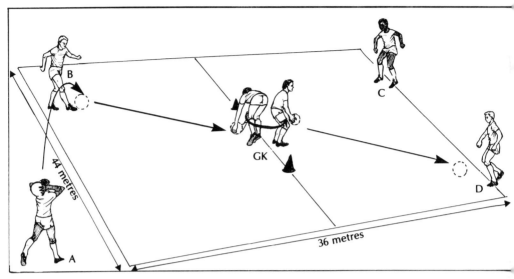

Drill 76

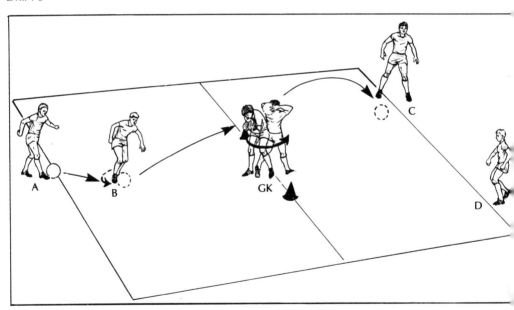

Drill 78

(80)   To complement shooting practice each player should do at least twelve penalty kicks.

Coaching Points

Shooting is an activity which requires care and planning in terms of space, unless you have a wall or fence behind the goal. Wit portable goals or markers, both sides of th goal can be used for practice and it is, c course, useful to combine the shooting wit practice for the goalkeeper.

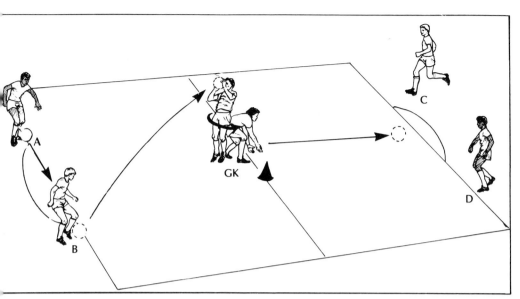

coach

(81)   You will need one full-size goal and a goalkeeper for this drill. There should be eight against eight in the penalty area and a supply of at least six footballs. In order to increase reaction speed to the options of shooting or dribbling, all practice takes place in the penalty area. The emphasis is 'can you shoot?' If your way is blocked, then dribble, or inter-pass, or shield the ball and pass it to someone who can shoot. When defenders win the ball they can either pass it to the goalkeeper, which helps them practise keeping calm, or pass it out to the coach. To keep the practice going the coach has a supply of spare balls ready to use. The aim is to score as many goals as possible in a fixed time or alternatively from twelve attempts. This practice generates much enthusiasm as the coach keeps asking each attacker 'can you shoot?' or telling each

defender 'do not let him shoot'. It also keep the goalkeeper busy and alert.

(82)   **Shooting and dribbling.** Practise thi drill in an area of fifty by forty metres; i needs two teams of eight (the two teams ar distinguished by different shirts which in thi case do not correspond to the key) and tw goalkeepers. Again the challenge is 'can yo shoot?' Practise dribbling in the attacking ha before attempting your shots.

(83)   Your practice should now progress t volley-shooting; when the ball has been playe forward into the attacking half the receivin attacker may pick the ball up and hand serv to a team-mate who must volley for goal Score two points for a goal from a volley. Thi practice helps to speed up a player's reactio to changes in thinking, as the service come from a variety of passes.

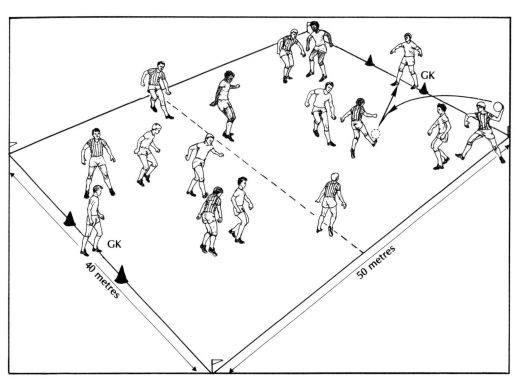

Drill 82

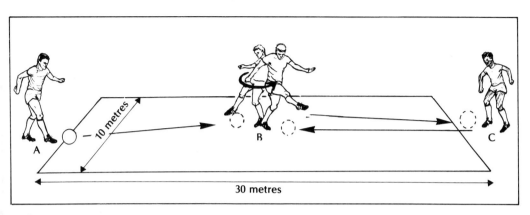

Drill 84

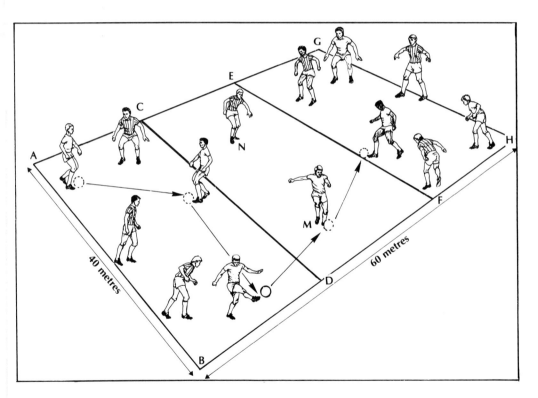

Drill 85

Practices for Midfield Players

(84)   **Turning and passing.** You will require three players in an area of thirty metres by ten metres. B receives a pass from A and controls it. Then B turns and passes to C, who returns the ball to B. On receiving the ball, B turns to pass to A. Do this continually for five minutes and then change positions. When in the central position try meeting the ball and turning with one touch, or spin on the ball and pass with the next touch.

(85)   You can vary these drills by using seven against seven in an area of sixty metres by forty metres. The aim is to make three or four consecutive passes in the teams of three before the ball is played to the midfield player M or N in area CDFE. The midfield player with the ball must then transfer the ball to team-mates in the box opposite to the one from which it came. If player M loses the ball to the other midfield player N, N then passes to colleagues in the other box; players must stay in their areas. Whilst players are waiting for the ball they must keep moving. Pressure can be relieved in the middle section, depending on the level of skill, by stipulating that there should be no contact in this section of the play.

(86)   Add one or two players to the basic Drill 85 in the middle section so that there are now two against two, or three against three, in area CDFE. Demand quick transfer through this section with two- or three-touch play allowed.

PRACTICES FOR GOALKEEPERS

This chapter would not be complete without reference to practices for goalkeepers. They are often forgotten or neglected during coaching or teaching sessions and left on their own to work out a training schedule. As a specialist player the goalkeeper can benefit from the combined practice with a colleague, whether that player is another goalkeeper or an outfield player.

A Goalkeeper Alone

Practice should preferably be on grass with at least one ball. If indoors you need to use plenty of landing mats in the goal area.

(87)   **Quality of movement.** The balanced movement of a goalkeeper is vital. Feet should be shoulder-width apart at all times if possible; whether moving forwards, sideways or backwards and when goalkeeping you should avoid bringing your feet together or placing them far apart. In order to 'take off' you must readjust your feet before doing so. Movement should be springy, on the balls of your feet and as light as a dancer, a boxer or a fencer. You should keep your body balanced and be ready to move in any direction. Only when you make the decision to act should you break out of this fundamental movement pattern or starting position. Then you can run, jump, dive – or whatever – in order to save the ball. Practise these movements without a ball to improve your technique.

Drill 87

(88)   Throw the ball up in the air. Run, then jump to catch the ball while it is as high as possible. Take off on one foot, keep your eyes on the ball. When you grasp the ball make sure your fingers are spread out with your thumbs at the back and side of the ball.

Drill 88

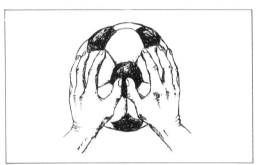

Drill 88

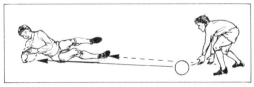

Drill 89

(89)   Roll the ball to your left or right; run and then dive for the ball. Aim to slide into the ball with your chest and then wrap your arms around it. Recover by getting to your feet and throw again.

Using a Wall

(90)   This is a very helpful facility for goal-keepers working on their own because the ball now approaches from in front of you. Throw the ball against the wall and stop the rebound by getting your body behind the ball to give 'double cover'.

Drill 90

Drill 90

Drill 90

(91) Kick the ball against the wall for increased power of rebound. This service will now be more unpredictable and you will need to react quickly in order to get your body behind the ball. Adjust your position nearer or further from the wall to make it easier or more difficult.

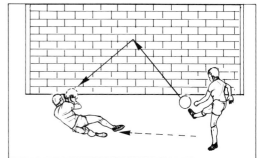

Drill 92

Coaching Points

Serving a ball against a wall and diving to save the rebound will need very good footwork. After kicking the ball at the wall with sufficient force, you will need to move your feet quickly in order to take off for the dive. This aids your reaction time and general ability in speeding up your movement. You should be improving the following techniques: good footwork, shot stopping, taking a high ball, diving to the left or right and coming to meet the ball.

Drills 93–96 require two goalkeepers, two goals (use cones) and a playing area of twenty metres square.

Drill 91

(92) **Diving.** Eventually you will find that there is insufficient time to get your feet, legs or body behind the ball and you will have to dive for the ball. You can dive and hold the ball or dive and push the ball away. Use the wall as before; but angle your shots so that you have to dive for the rebound, making random serves using your hands and feet. Serve to the left and right to avoid developing a strong side preference. Remember when you dive to leave the ground and to look at the ball between your arms, keeping the top arm out of the way of your vision.

(93) A throws or kicks the ball to B so that B can practise shot stopping. Eventually change positions. This should involve a variety of saves as the shots will vary in power and in distance reached.

(94) **Leaving the line.** A rolls the ball to B, so that B needs to advance towards A. As soon as B touches the ball A leaves his line and comes out to challenge B. B should shoot whenever he or she can for A to save. Take it in turns to be attacker and goalkeeper.

(95) Vary Drill 94 by B dribbling straight towards you so that as the goalkeeper you can practise coming out to the attacker's feet. As you go down to B's feet, 'hit' the ball with your chest. Slide into the ball, but do not dive.

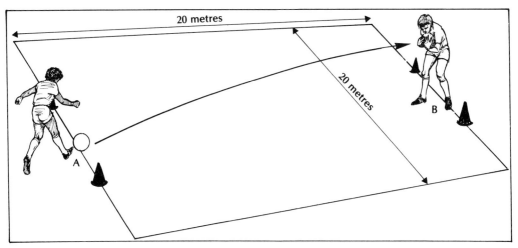

Drill 93

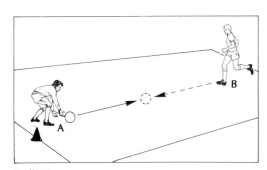

Drill 94

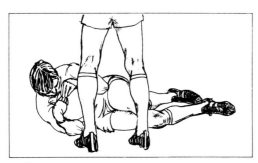

Drill 95

Clamp your arms round the ball and as soon as you have the ball curl up for protection. As you were sliding towards the attacker, your body should have been 'long' in order to cover as much of the goal as possible. Be single-minded and look for the ball at all times.

(96) A passes to B. B dribbles towards A's goal and tries to score a goal. A must combine all the goalkeeping practices, ensuring that any decisions will be good – imagine that you are playing in a match.

Coaching Points

The goalkeeper must make decisions such as: 'are my angles correct?'(*see* Diagram M), 'how far dare I go without being lobbed?', 'has the player lost control of the ball?', 'can I stay on my feet for as long as possible?'

The basic decisions facing a goalkeeper will be:

(i) can you get to the ball when it is played far in front of the attacker or when the attacker has lost control?

(ii) are your approach angles good?

(iii) are you determined to get the ball?

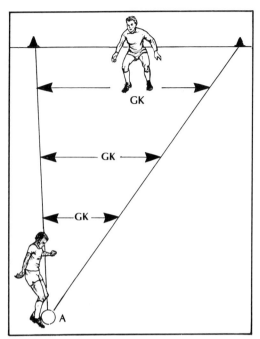

Diagram M

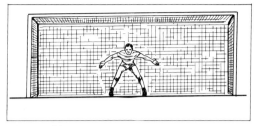

Diagram N

(see Diagram M), covering as much as possible of the goal-mouth. Crouch in a position of readiness, making your body as big as possible by spreading your arms (see Diagram N). Come as far out as you dare, remembering the attacker may chip or lob the ball over you or swerve the ball round you. Be prepared to rush to the attacker's feet if control is lost or to stop the likely shot on goal.

This is a cat and mouse game and you are the cat. Generally speaking, the goal-keeper should try to put the attacker under pressure, but there is little point in rushing at a forward player who has good control of the ball.

Taking High Crosses

For Drills 97 and 98 you need two goal-keepers, two or more footballs and a fixed or portable goal.

Remember that when you leave the goal-mouth you *must* make contact with the ball. If you decide not to go down to the player's feet, you must make a correct angle with your posts

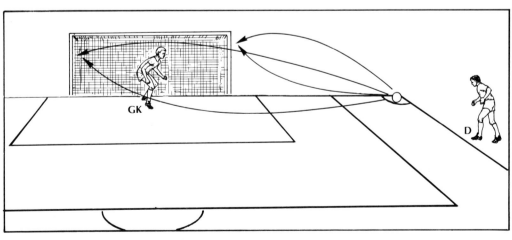

Drill 97

(97) Player D crosses, by throwing or kicking, into the penalty area. These should include near-post and far-post centres and inswinging and outswinging trajectories. The goalkeeper should start in the middle of the goal in a position of readiness.

Coaching Points

The near-post cross will not give you much time, so be ready to attack the ball at the near post. Take the ball when it is as high as possible with one continuous movement. Do not start too soon as this may mean that you get under the ball or, worse still, finish up moving backwards to adjust your position.

(98) Continue Drill 97 with D placing the ball at the far post. The goalkeeper should make one movement across the arc of the ball and take it high at A, B or C.

Coaching Points

Far-post crosses allow more time for you to adjust your feet and make a good decision (generally about three seconds). You should therefore have time to move at least eight to

ten yards since three seconds can allow you to move as much as fifteen metres. You can never practise high crosses too much since it is the one aspect of goalkeeping skills that distinguishes the very good (or excellent) from the average. It is largely a matter of timing, which cannot be taught. However, you can be taught all the techniques, although on the match day you still have to make the decision as to which technique to use and when to act.

Whenever possible you need to practise catching high crosses in a crowded penalty area, but this, of course, has to be part of team preparation. A good maxim for high crosses is; 'wait a fraction longer'. You can always accelerate forwards, but to be caught moving backwards, or on a standing jump under the ball, could be disastrous.

Free Kicks and Penalties

(99) You require a fixed goal, four bollards and penalty-area markings. With only one player to work with, a 'wall' of sorts can be made with posts or large bollards. Set them up on side X or Y. See how many yards nearer to the ball you can get as the forward runs up to shoot. Take care to be still as he strikes the ball

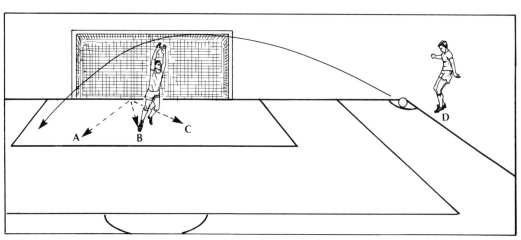

Drill 98

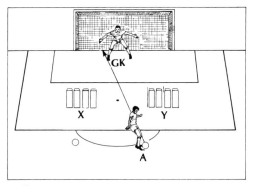

Drill 99

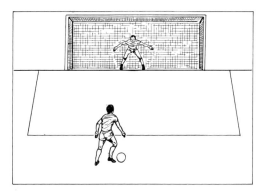

Drill 100

and be in your position of readiness. Do not go too far or the ball could be chipped or lobbed over you. Be determined to save the shot and keep your concentration on the ball at all times.

Penalties

(100)   For this drill you need a fixed goal and two players. Practise the position of readiness; in this situation you must be quite still, with your feet on the goal-line. Your weight should be on the balls of your feet with your knees flexed and turned slightly inward so that you are ready to dive in either direction. Take sets of twelve penalties each, watching the ball and not the kicker.

Coaching Points

Although the law says that a goalkeeper shall not move until the penalty is kicked, the interpretation of this law seems to allow a goalkeeper to sway from the hips. This movement may suggest to the penalty-taker that the goalkeeper is going to move left or right and is often part of the game of bluff in which the goalkeeper and the penalty-taker engage. This is all part of the psychology of the game because it is chiefly concerned with decision-making and so is beyond the scope of this chapter.

2 Physical Fitness

The constant rise in standards in sport can be attributed to many things, such as improved techniques and equipment. What heights, for example, would pole-vaulters manage without fibre-glass poles? However, in some sports the equipment is relatively unimportant and the techniques may not have changed much. What, then, can account for improvement in these sports? Quite probably the key factor is *physical fitness*. Not only does it contribute to the end result in soccer, but it is now recognised that fitness is a very important part of training. Indeed fitness is important at all levels of the game, for while it is essential for international competition it is also beneficial for beginners, improving both their effectiveness and enjoyment of the game.

WHAT IS PHYSICAL FITNESS?

Physical fitness involves a multitude of components, so making it difficult to see fitness as one single thing. In fact when people ask how fit you are, they are asking a rather naive question. If I was asked the same type of question about my car, I might say that it is excellent for comfort, good on motorways, not very good for acceleration and in need of improvement when starting in the wet! An overall comment on how good (fit) my car is depends on which aspect is being referred to.

Similarly, we can refer to many different parts, or components, of fitness. Nowadays there is a great deal of interest in fitness for health, which includes exercises for stamina (such as jogging), posture, weight control and so on. Fitness for sport will include some of these components as well as others, such as speed and power. The importance of each

component for your sport obviously depends upon the sport itself. Soccer is a dynamic all-round game requiring most types of fitness. However, you can imagine the marathon runner and weight-lifter having, for the most part, quite different fitness training programmes.

The components of physical fitness for sport which require physical training are summarised in Fig 1. As you can see, these components are cardiorespiratory fitness (stamina), muscular endurance, strength, power, speed and flexibility. Many years ago sports coaches used to refer to the main components of fitness as the 'six Ss' – stamina, strength, speed, suppleness, skill and (p)sychology! One could easily add mental fitness, diet and nutrition, injury prevention and other areas to Fig 1.

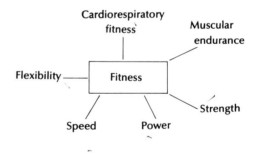

Fig 1 A model of physical fitness for sport.

However, the diagram refers to the main components of fitness which require physical activity and cause changes in the physiological state of the body.

Finally, regarding the definition of fitness; it is sometimes claimed that fitness is a set of attributes that individuals have or achieve and which help in their ability to perform physical activity. The phrase 'have or achieve' is interesting since it suggests that fitness in sport is dependent on two things: natural ability ('have') and training ('achieve'). Many aspects of fitness are governed by our heredity, yet with training we are able to make the most of what we have. Unfortunately, 750cc Fiats will never race in Formula One events. However, you may enjoy racing a good 750cc Fiat if it is given the right care and attention, especially if you compete against cars of the same type. Indeed, with good maintenance (training) the 750cc Fiat will be able to beat a less well maintained car with a larger engine as it may possess other superior qualities rather than just power.

PRINCIPLES OF FITNESS TRAINING

Regardless of the fitness component we are talking about, certain basic principles apply to all aspects of fitness training in soccer. These are:

(i)   frequency;
(ii)   intensity;
(iii)   progressive overload;
(iv)   time;
(v)   type (of exercise);
(vi)   specificity;
(vii)   reversibility.

Frequency

Frequency refers to the number of training sessions during a particular period of time, usually the number of sessions per week. Most sports require two or three although obviously those people striving for the highest honours will train much more frequently. (Indeed, many sports today require their top athletes to train several times a day!) However, for most people, a significant improvement in fitness can be made with at least three sessions each week.

Intensity

This refers to how hard the athlete trains. This will differ greatly between individuals, although similar training programmes can be performed on a relative basis. This means, for example, that two athletes can perform three sets of five repetitions of the leg-press exercise in the weight-training room at 75 per cent of their maximum. However, the actual weight lifted may differ considerably. Superior athletes with an extensive training background are also likely to be able to train at a higher level for longer and recover more quickly. The intensity of your training will have a major effect on how effective it is. Too little intensity will not produce much of an effect, but too much intensity is likely to lead to injury and fatigue. For these reasons, the principle of *progressive overload* is important (*see* Fig 2).

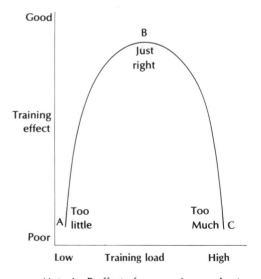

Note A→B effect of progressive overload

Fig 2   Progressive overload.

Progressive Overload

The old story of Milo carrying a calf on his shoulders is the perfect illustration of progressive overload. Milo started off carrying a small calf but as the animal grew in size and weight, Milo did not find it progressively more difficult to carry. Instead, he adapted to the increasing load as his muscles grew stronger. Eventually, he could carry a fully-grown bull. Two things are important here: first, Milo was *progressive* in his training; he gradually adapted to the increasing load. Imagine what would have happened if he tried to lift the bull having had several months of inactivity! Second, Milo adapted to the load through *overload*. This is a fundamental mechanism since, with increased training, the body will either adapt and grow (with sensible progressive overload) or collapse (through inappropriate training – 'too much too soon'). This is illustrated in Fig 2.

Time

This simply refers to the amount of time spent in a training session. This will vary greatly depending on the sport and the individual, but most fitness training sessions, allowing for an adequate warm-up and cool-down, last at least forty minutes.

Type (of Exercise)

Fitness training sessions will vary in terms of the type of exercise used. Some sessions will contain predominantly cardiorespiratory exercises, others strength and flexibility etc. This will depend, again, on the individual and the sport in question. For example, the fitness requirements of the goalkeeper will clearly differ from those of the midfield player.

You may have noticed that the above concepts can be easily remembered by using the word FITT, the letters stand for frequency, intensity (including overload), time and type.

This 'FITT principle' forms the corner-stone for many sports' fitness-training programmes. However, there are other basic principles to remember.

Specificity

Ultimately the aim of your fitness training must be to make you a better footballer. It may be very satisfying to improve your best time for running a three-mile course, but if it does not help your soccer it is misplaced effort. Fitness training, therefore, should be specific to the sport in question. However, this does not mean that the fundamental components of fitness are ignored. It would be pointless to train for hours every day to improve your neck strength for heading if you lack the fundamental speed to get to the ball first! A combination of exercise is therefore required.

Reversibility

'Use it or lose it!' is a common expression in sport. Unless you continue training, the fitness you have built up will be lost quite quickly. Some people seem to retain their fitness better than others but these individuals probably have a high natural ability to perform, as mentioned earlier. They will still lose the effects of training if they fail to continue, but the effects may not appear to be so marked. A run-down Formula One car will still beat a well-tuned 750cc Fiat!

COMPONENTS OF FITNESS FOR SOCCER

Soccer is a fast game requiring players to develop all of the qualities outlined in Fig 1. However, some of these components are considered more important than others. Fig 3 is a guide to the relative importance of each fitness component in soccer. The purpose of this section of the chapter, therefore, is to outline

Fitness components	Important	Very Important
Cardiorespiratory Fitness	—	●
Muscular Endurance	●	—
Strength	●	—
Power	—	●
Speed (and agility)	—	●
Flexibility	●	—

Fig 3   Fitness components for soccer.

each of these components and show how they can be developed to maximise their effectiveness in football. Before these components are considered, it is important to say something about the warm-up.

Warm-Up

An important part of the training process, the warm-up is a period of exercise performed prior to the main part of the training session or game. It is used to prepare the body for subsequent vigorous action and can be divided into two main phases: general warm-up and sport-specific warm-up.

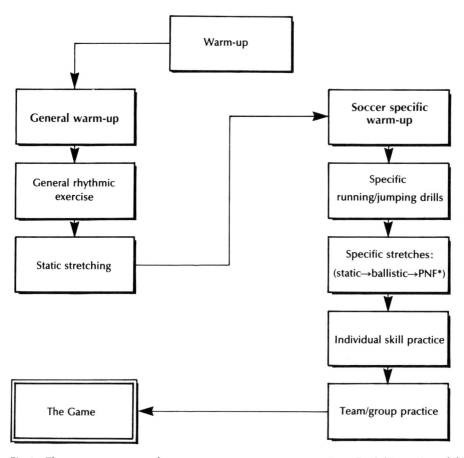

Fig 4   The warm-up process for soccer.

* *see* flexibility section of this chapter

The general warm-up should consist of the following exercises: gentle rhythmic 'total body' exercises, such as jogging or callisthenics which should slowly increase in intensity and produce a slight sweat and raised pulse and secondly static stretching exercises (*see* the flexibility section later in this chapter).

The sport-specific part of the warm-up, as the name suggests, should include exercises which specifically prepare you for your game, such as jumping exercises for heading, twisting movements and jumping for goalkeepers, wind-up sprints for outfield players and so on. These can then be followed by practising the skills themselves. The warm-up process for soccer is summarised in Fig 4.

In addition to preparing to *start* activity, you should also prepare to finish! This is done by cooling down after periods of vigorous activity with exercises similar to those used to warm up, such as gentle rhythmic exercises and stretching. In fact, this is a particularly good time for stretching as your muscles will be warm and so very receptive to this form of exercise.

CARDIORESPIRATORY FITNESS

Let us first try to understand the terminology. Cardiorespiratory (CR) fitness is also known as cardiovascular fitness, aerobic exercise, stamina fitness and probably a host of other names. For our purposes cardiorespiratory fitness is probably good enough and it is achieved through the stamina-type exercises associated with activities such as cycling, jogging and swimming. The local muscular endurance fitness needed in exercises like sit-ups or press-ups is, of course, very much related to cardiorespiratory fitness since it is the CR system that is responsible for getting oxygen to the working muscles. However, specific local muscular endurance is considered separately since many different exercises can be prescribed for this component.

Physiologists have known for a long time that the body operates through different types of energy systems. For example, strikers require shorter bursts of higher intensity effort while midfield players need more prolonged effort often at a slightly lower intensity. The three main energy systems are summarised in Fig 5. From this you will see that CR fitness, or stamina, is associated with the aerobic energy system. The word aerobic means 'with air' (or oxygen) and is applied to continuous activities in which the oxygen that is breathed in is sufficient to supply the energy required for that particular activity – so walking is an aerobic form of exercise and sprinting is an-aerobic (without oxygen/air), as high-speed sprinting cannot be sustained for long (*see* Fig 5). Anaerobic training will be considered later in this chapter.

Aerobic Endurance

Aerobic CR fitness is developed by progressively taxing the CR system (the heart, lungs, blood vessels and the blood itself) and so the most practical indication of aerobic training intensity is the heart rate, or pulse. It is generally thought that gains in CR fitness will occur when the heart rate (HR) is raised to a sufficient level for a 'training effect'. But what is a sufficient level? As a general rule optimal gains in CR fitness occur when the HR is raised to within 60–90 per cent of maximum, where maximum is estimated as 220 minus your age (in years). This figure gives the number of beats per minute. For example:

Person: A. Robic
Age   : 20 years
Estimated maximum HR:
220 – 20   = 200 beats/minute (bpm)
Training zone = 60–90% of max
              = 120–180 bpm

This is likely to yield a conservative estimate at the lower end of the range for most active

	ENERGY SYSTEMS		
	1	**2**	**3**
Duration	0–15 secs	15 secs–2 mins	Over 2 mins
Technical term	ATP–PC system	LA (lactic acid)	Aerobic system
Description	Strength, power speed	Short-term muscular endurance	Long-term muscular endurance and aerobic activity
Soccer activities	Short sprint for ball	Continuous attack	Prolonged 'open play'; recovery between plays

ATP = adenosine triphosphate
PC = phosphocreatine

Fig 5   The main energy systems of the body and their practical meaning in soccer.

FITT Component	Minimum criteria
Frequency	3 times per week
Intensity	Elevated heart rate between 60–90% of maximum, or 220 − (age +25) beats per minute
Time	20 minutes
Type (of exercise)	Gross body exercise, such as running, swimming, cycling

Fig 6   The FITT principle applied to aerobic cardiorespiratory training.

sports people, so another simpler method is to add 25 to your age and subtract the sum from 220.

Person: A. Robic
Age   : 20 years
CR training intensity
= 220 − (20+25)
= 220 − 45
= 175 bpm

You can count your own pulse either at your wrist or your neck. At the wrist (the radial pulse) simply place three fingers (not your thumb) lightly on your up-turned wrist at the base of the thumb. It is probably easier to count for fifteen seconds and then multiply by four for your bpm figure. Errors will occur but these should diminish with practice. A stronger pulse can be felt at the neck (the carotid pulse) by placing the fingers gently against the neck at the base of the angle of the jaw bone. For reasons of safety, you must not press too hard.

Fig 6 summarises the FITT principle for aerobic fitness training. This shows minimum criteria and many active sportspeople will require greater levels of training. Moreover, for maximum benefit in the game of football the types of exercise used should be as relevant and similar to the game as possible. This suggests that swimming and cycling will not be as good for the soccer player as running, and indeed running might best be done in 'interval' form to simulate the stop-start action of the game itself. However, it is important to remember that the CR system is central to recovery from all forms of exercise, so although some players (goalkeepers, for example) need not have the running endurance of the long-distance athlete, they do need a fundamental base of adequate aerobic fitness.

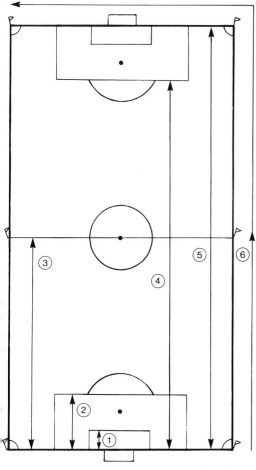

Fig 7   Aerobic training using the soccer field.

A variety of aerobic-type running drills will be well-known to many players and coaches. Fig 7 shows how the pitch markings can be used to vary the distances of aerobic shuttle-running exercises. Longer distances for prolonged periods of time (routes 4, 5 and 6) may be more applicable to midfield players, while the defensive backs need shorter runs (routes 1, 2 and 3) but run at a faster pace. Both sets of exercises can be primarily aerobic if the activity is fairly continuous and the heart rate elevated throughout. Progressive overload can be achieved by requiring a faster time for the run, or by reducing the rest periods. The drills given in Chapter 1 can also be incorporated. This combination is useful because:

(i)   it provides a form of training similar to the actual game;
(ii)   players can immediately see the point of the activity;
(iii)   it allows for variety in fitness training.

However, caution needs to be exercised since the load placed on the player should not be so great that it causes the skills to be performed badly; fatigue is a major cause of skill breakdown – so beware.

Assessing Aerobic Fitness

The best way to use fitness tests is to compare scores over a period of time for the same player thereby tracking his or her progress. Simple field tests can be used, such as recording the distance run around a track in twelve minutes, the time taken to run one and a half miles and so on. Assuming that the conditions (including the motivation of the player), stay the same from one test to the next, changes in scores will give some indication of changing fitness levels. Another simple indication is to step up and down on a bench or stair approximately fifty centimetres high (although the exact height does not greatly matter). Perform for a set time, perhaps five minutes, to a

Term	Definition
Strength	The maximum force that a muscle, or group of muscles, can generate. Sometimes the statement 'at a specified speed or velocity' can be added to this definition because force will diminish as the speed of the limb increases.
Muscular endurance	The ability of the muscle or muscle group to continue applying force.
Power	The product of force and velocity. In simpler terms, therefore, is strength x speed.
Flexibility	Range of motion about a joint or series of joints.

Fig 8   Definition of terms applied to muscle fitness.

definite rhythm or beat and then take your pulse. If this exercise is repeated at a later date in exactly the same way any changes in the pulse give some indication of CR fitness changes. Such simple methods can be appealing but are only rough guides to progress. With the growing availability of laboratory testing, more accurate measures should be possible for a greater number of players.

The area of 'muscle fitness' will be considered next, but before proceeding, you should check the definitions of these terms in Fig 8. These different components of muscle fitness are often interrelated. For example, in order to develop power both strength and speed are necessary. For the sake of simplicity, however, most areas will be considered separately, but you should bear in mind the overlap that does exist.

MUSCULAR ENDURANCE

This aspect of fitness follows on naturally from aerobic fitness. Since muscular endurance is the ability to repeat muscle contractions — such as repetition sit-ups — over time, improving this component of fitness requires a relatively high number of repetitions to be

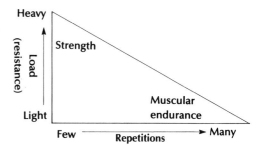

Fig 9   The strength-muscular endurance continuum.

performed. This is the reverse of strength development, as explained later and illustrated in Fig 9. It is clearly the case that large numbers of repetitions can only be performed with a relatively small resistance. While this may be external resistance, such as weights, it is often sufficient simply to use body-weight, such as in press-ups and sit-ups. A series of basic body-weight endurance exercises is shown in Figs 10 and 11.

More specific application to soccer can be made by constant repetition of certain game skills. However, care should be taken that the skills are replicated exactly. Some soccer-related exercises are shown in the section on strength development.

Name	Figure	Muscle action
Press-ups	11(i)	Back of upper arms (triceps) and chest
Pull-ups	11(ii)	Front of upper arms (biceps), shoulders and upper back
Sit-ups	11(iii)	Stomach
Back extensions	11(iv)	Back muscles

Note: leg muscles may require additional resistance. (*See* the leg exercises shown in the weight-training section of this chapter). People sometimes refer to 'pull-ups' as involving an over-grasp grip and 'chins' an undergrasp grip. The effect is similar. You should always perform sit-ups with bent legs and for back extensions you should not lift your shoulders far above your hips.

Fig 10   Basic body-weight muscular endurance exercises.

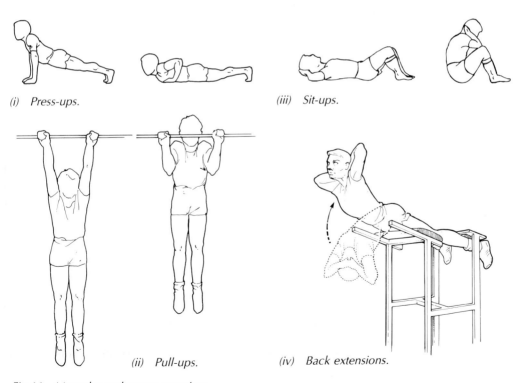

(i)   *Press-ups.*

(iii)   *Sit-ups.*

(ii)   *Pull-ups.*

(iv)   *Back extensions.*

Fig 11   Muscular endurance exercises.

Assessing Muscular Endurance

Basic tests of muscular endurance are simple to perform, although they always depend on the subject performing at maximum effort and motivation. As with the CR tests, you can use them to plot individual progress. Any muscular endurance exercise can be used as a test as long as it can be easily measured – for example, the number of sit-ups performed in a set time. Of course, comparisons are only valid if the techniques are always the same.

STRENGTH AND POWER

No other area of physical fitness has suffered more than strength training from misunderstanding and mythology. The 'circus strongman' image still persists in many instances, but it is just as easy to find slim 800m runners lifting weights as is it heavily-built shot-putters. Weight training, the most common strength training method, is simply a way of increasing the resistance placed on the muscles to stimulate their growth and development. Whilst on this subject, some popular misconceptions need correction: women will *not* become masculine if they lift weights; it is *not* possible

for muscle to turn into fat; weight training will *not* slow you down. Indeed modern-day athletes use strength and power training extensively, although it must be said that some sports are more advanced in their methods than others. In short, there is no dynamic sport where some form of resistance training is not required.

Before proceeding, it is worth looking again at Fig 8. Very few sports involve maximum force at slow speeds – most require fast strength (power), however, because power is a combination of strength and speed, the two terms will be dealt with together while pure speed will be considered separately.

Without going into great detail on how muscles actually work, it is worth noting briefly that there are different types of muscle fibre. 'Slow-twitch' (ST or type I) fibres, as their name suggests, are endurance fibres with low power. The 'fast-twitch' (FT or type II) fibres are the opposite – powerful but only able to operate briefly.

In fact, there are two subdivisions of these fast twitch muscle fibres; type IIa fibres and IIb fibres. The latter has a very fast twitch action while IIa fibres, although having a fast twitch action also have some endurance capacity. We all possess both ST and FT fibres in

Characteristics	Slow Twitch	Fast Twitch
Aerobic capacity	High	Low
Anaerobic capacity	Low	High
Contraction time	Slow	Fast
Force	Low	High
Activities	Endurance-type	Sprint/explosive-type
Fatigue	Slow	Fast

Fig 12   Summary of characteristics of fast and slow-twitch muscle fibres, adapted from Fox, E.L., Sports Physiology *(Saunders College, 1979).*

varying proportions, the ratio being determined by heredity. However, through a process of self selection it is likely that marathon runners will have a high percentage of ST fibres and sprinters a high percentage of FT fibres, although there is probably great variation within these two extreme groups. Fig 12 summarises the differences between the two main types of fibres, and Fig 13 illustrates the order in which the fibres are always recruited.

This order (type I, type IIa, type IIb) and the associated intensity of exercise needed to bring about this recruitment show that heavy resistance and high intensity training (high loads with repetitions of six or less) is probably the best way to develop explosive strength. This contradicts the commonly held belief that heavy resistance training will slow you down. Once repetitions start to exceed about six, the initial tension on the muscle is reduced and fewer type IIb fibres are recruited. However, fast movements with lower resistances can also be used to recruit fast-twitch fibres. In short, exercise must be of an intense nature to recruit FT fibres, and this may include heavy resistance work previously thought to be detrimental for games players.

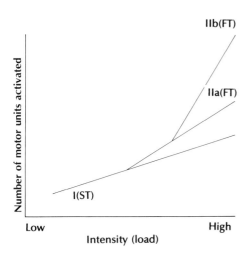

Fig 13   Recruitment pattern of muscle fibres.

Types of Strength and Power Training Methods

There are several different ways of developing your strength and these are the following.

(i) Constant resistance (sometimes called isotonic); this is the conventional type of training involving barbells, dumb-bells and bodyweight. Although called constant resistance, this is slightly inaccurate as the actual resistance on the muscle will change as the body levers create different forces (the weight on the bar, of course, does remain the same). This is probably the most accessible form of effective strength training for soccer players.
(ii) Static resistance (isometric); force is applied to an immovable object and so no movement is observed. This, however, is not a very useful form of training for soccer players because of its static nature and can also be unsafe for older people as it creates sharp elevations in blood pressure.
(iii) Same-speed training (isokinetic); performed with the aid of a machine which will only allow the limb to move at a set speed. The resistance on the muscle depends on the voluntary effort of the athlete. This training benefits water sports and requires special machines, such as isokinetic swim benches.
(iv) Variable resistance; performed on machines which vary the resistance put on the muscle through its whole range of movement. This helps overcome the inherent weakness of isotonic training in which the muscle is only working at maximal force in one part of the range of movement. However, variable resistance machines are still not readily available to all athletes and tend only to cater for single-joint actions. Since most sports demand multi-jointed actions, a combination of isotonic and variable resistance exercise is desirable.

Exercises can, of course, be differentiated according to the part of the body you wish to develop, such as lower, middle and upper.

However, in addition to this it is worth splitting the exercises into three function types; general, specific and competition-specific.

General strength/power exercises are required by almost all sportspeople for basic increases in strength and power in the major muscle groups of the body, such as the legs, back and shoulders. Specific exercises are those which work the muscles particularly relevant to the sport in question, in this case football and competition-specific are those resistance exercises which copy, as closely as possible, the skills needed in the actual sport. For example, exercises for soccer players might include jumping with ankle weights attached. Figs 14, 15 and 16 suggest some resistance exercises for each of these categories. The exercises are illustrated in Figs 17 –29 and Figs 30–32 explain how they should be performed.

Exercise	Major muscles involved	Equipment	Figure
Power clean	Hips, legs, back (power development)	Barbell	17
Front squat	Hips, legs (quadriceps)	Barbell	18
Leg extension	Quadriceps	Machine	19
Leg curl	Hamstrings	Machine	20
Side bends	Oblique (side) abdominals	Dumb-bell	21
Bench press	Chest, triceps, shoulders	Barbell or Machine	22
Arm curl	Biceps	Barbell or Machine	23

Fig 14   General resistance exercises for soccer players.

Exercise	Major muscles involved	Equipment	Figure
Split squats	Quadriceps (and for hip flexibility)	Barbell	24
Dumb-bell jump squats	Quadriceps, hips	Dumb-bells	25
Plyometric exercises	Hips, quadriceps, calves	Benches/gym boxes	26

Fig 15   Specific resistance exercises for soccer players.

Exercise	Major muscles involved	Simulation of	Equipment	Figure
Neck exercises	Neck	Heading	None	27
Resistance running	Quadriceps, hips, calves	Sprinting; breaking tackles	Belt, rope	28
Crouching dumb-bell press	Triceps, shoulders, quadriceps, hips	Jumping to head ball	Dumb-bells	29

Fig 16   Competition-specific resistance exercises for soccer players.

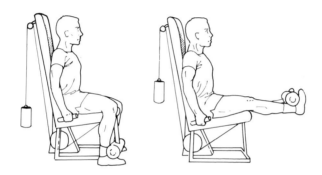

Fig 17   Power clean.

Fig 18   Front squat.

Fig 19   Leg extension.

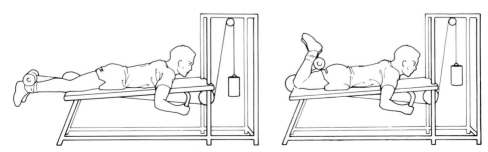

Fig 20   Leg curl.

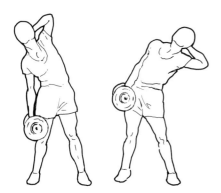

Fig 21   Side bends.

Fig 22   Bench press.

Fig 23   Arm curl.

Fig 24   Split squats.

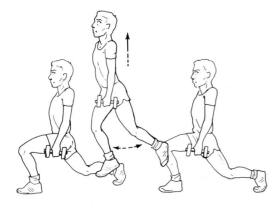

Fig 25   Dumb-bell jump squats.

Fig 26   Plyometric exercises.

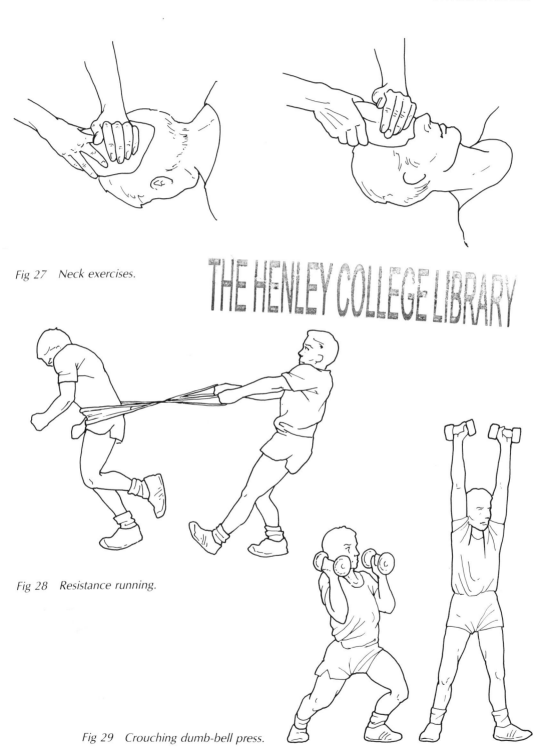

Fig 27   Neck exercises.

THE HENLEY COLLEGE LIBRARY

Fig 28   Resistance running.

Fig 29   Crouching dumb-bell press.

Figure	Exercise	Starting position	Movement	Other points
17	Power clean	Feet under bar, hip-width apart. Shoulder-width overgrasp grip. Hips below shoulders. Arms straight, back flat.	Lift bar from floor with straight arms and keep back flat. Extend body. Keep bar close in. Turn wrists over and receive bar on front of shoulders. Bend legs to receive bar. Lower to thighs, then to floor.	Have bar 20 cm off the floor to start with. Use blocks or wooden disks for this. Make movement smooth and, later, fast and dynamic.
18	Front squat	Bar on chest, high elbows. Feet flat just outside hip-width.	Squat under control to 'thighs parallel'. Return to standing. Keep chest up throughout.	Avoid deep ballistic squatting.
19	Leg extension	Feet under lower pads. Sit upright.	Extend legs; lower under control.	
20	Leg curl	Face down on machine, heels under top pads.	Bring heels up towards buttocks. Return under control.	
21	Side bends	Stand with feet beyond hip-width. Dumb-bell in one hand at the side, other hand behind head or at the side.	Bend sideways with weight, return to middle position and beyond to position of stretch. Return to start.	Move sideways only. Do not use a dumb-bell in each hand.
22	Bench press	Lie face up on a bench. Hips, shoulders, head all on bench. Shoulder-width grip of bar.	Lower bar to chest. Extend arms until fully straightened.	If using a barbell rather than machine, beginners may find it easier to balance if they start the exercise with the bar on the chest.
23	Arm curl	Undergrasp grip on bar; upright body.	Pull bar to top of the chest, keeping elbows at the side of the body. Return under control.	

Note: although specific breathing techniques can be recommended for each exercise, it is often easier, particularly with beginners, simply to suggest that they breathe freely and naturally. Do *not* hold your breath during the execution of these exercises. This applies to all the exercises in Figs 17–32.

Fig 30   Explanation of general weight-training exercises.

Figure	Exercise	Starting position	Movement	Other points
24	Split squats	Bar on front shoulders, elbows high. Feet split front–back. Front foot flat, toes pointing slightly inwards. Rear foot on toes, pointing forwards.	Bend front leg and push hips down and forward. Maintain upright trunk. Push back off front leg once thigh is parallel to floor.	Repeat exercise with other foot forwards.
25	Dumb-bell jump squats	Dumb-bell in each hand, stand with one foot in front of the other – legs bent.	Leap into the air, reverse foot position and land by bending the legs.	
26	Plyometric exercises	These are bounding-type exercises with or without boxes for varying the height and depth of jumps.		

Fig 31   Explanation of specific resistance exercises.

Figure	Exercise	Starting position	Movement	Other points
27	Neck exercises	A variety of resistance exercises for the neck can be attempted; see Fig 27		
28	Resistance running		Normal sprint/run action.	Ensure normal running action does not deteriorate with excessive resistance.
29	Crouching dumb-bell press	Feet front and back. Dumb-bell in each hand at shoulder height.	Extend legs and arms. Return under control.	

Fig 32   Explanation of competition-specific resistance exercises.

Planning Strength and Power Training

You should always remember that strength and power training is merely an aid to improved performance in soccer. The training should therefore be 'cycled' so that the maximum benefit is derived. This is a complex matter but limited space allows only a brief discussion. Basically, the strength/power training should develop across three phases of the year, starting at the end of the season. After a brief rest the player should start a basic strength programme, which should be largely made up from those exercises from Fig 14. As the new season approaches, the training should become more dynamic and power-oriented. Exercises from Fig 15 can now be added along with the competition-specific exercises as the first game draws closer. During the season itself, the number of sessions may be reduced perhaps from three to two per week, as the aim now is power maintenance. This process is shown in

	TIME		
	Preparation phase (out of season)	**Pre-competitive phase (pre-season)**	**Competitive phase (during season)**
Emphasis	Strength	Power	Power maintenance
Loading (intensity)	High	High	Medium
Exercises	Mainly general	General plus specific (some competition-specific	Mainly specific and competition-specific
Frequency	2–3 times per week	2–3 times per week	2 times per week
Time (excluding warm-up and cool-down)	45–60mins	40mins	30mins

Fig 33   Developing strength and power across the training year.

Fig 33. Using part of the FITT principle, the following guidelines can be offered to vary the training according to the individual:

(i)   Beginner (with weight training)
        Frequency: 2–3 times per week.
        Intensity: low; all weights should be light enough to perform 8–10 repetitions in good style, 3 sets each exercise.
        Time: initially short, 30 mins, but could increase to 45 mins.

(ii)   Intermediate
        Frequency: 2–3 times per week.
        Intensity: medium, occasionally high. Last few reps should be fairly hard (5 sets of 5 reps).
        Time: up to 1 hour.

(iii)   Advanced
        Frequency: 3–4 times per week.
        Intensity: varied, including *occasional* maximums.
        Time: up to 1 hour.

The structure of each session should be in the following order:

(i)   warm-up;
(ii)   general exercises;
(iii)   specific/competition-specific exercises;
(iv)   cool-down.

Needs Assessment

In their excellent book (*Designing Resistance Training Programmes,* 1987) giving advice on designing resistance training programmes, Fleck & Kraemer list a variety of important factors that should be assessed in planning a strength/power programme for an athlete. The three major 'needs assessment' categories identified were; exercise movements, metabolism used and injury prevention:

(i) Exercise movements. The coach, in planning the strength/power programmes for the players needs to know: which specific muscles and muscle groups have to be developed, whether there are any specific joint angles that need strengthening, what the emphasis should be in terms of strength, power, endurance etc. and finally, which type of exercise or exercises should be used (whether isotonic, isometric, isokinetic and so on).

(ii) Metabolism. You need to know what the estimated percentage contribution from each of the three main energy systems outlined in Fig 5 will be.

(iii) Injury. You also need to develop the most common sites of possible injury and select exercises suitable for sites of previous injuries.

Most of these factors require specialist weight-training coaches (such as those qualified through the British Amateur Weight Lifters' Association (BAWLA) scheme), working in close co-operation with football coaches.

Assessing Strength and Power

Assessing strength and power is often recommended by coaches and fitness experts but the measurement of strength can be a problem, particularly for beginners who are unused to maximum muscular effort. Moreover, this form of exercise may be dangerous for the inexperienced athlete. Also, some exercises require the learning of considerable skills before the athlete should attempt one repetition at maximum resistance. Although safer forms of strength testing (such as grip-strength tests) do exist, they are of limited value in most sports contexts. It is more advantageous to assess power and, in the case of soccer, leg power.

Fortunately, measuring leg power is relatively easy, although, as with all field tests of fitness, it gives only a rough indication of the fitness component. Two tests are well known: the standing long jump and the standing vertical jump (see Fig 34). These can be used to gauge the likely effectiveness of certain players in, for example, defensive heading. The jump tests can also be used to measure progress in the resistance training programme – improvements in leg power should occur after such a programme.

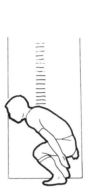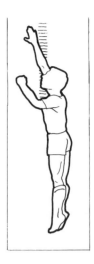

Fig 34   Vertical-jump test.

Additional Considerations in Strength and Power Training

Safety

Weight-training has an excellent safety record – particularly so when weight-trainers lift in a well-planned environment with good supervision. Nevertheless, like most activities, a safety code should be adhered to. The following are the main points to note:

Personal safety
(i)   learn correct techniques;
(ii)   train with other people so they can help out if necessary;
(iii)   warm up properly;
(iv)   wear appropriate clothing, including training shoes;
(v)   progress gradually through a planned schedule.

External safety
(i)   check all apparatus before use;

(ii)   keep all apparatus well maintained and clean;
(iii)   ensure the floor space is free of obstacles, such as loose disks etc;
(iv)   plan the floor space for maximum, but safe, use;
(v)   determine the maximum number of people who can use the facility safely and do not exceed this number.

Children's safety

When encouraging youngsters into sport it is always tempting to give them the same training programme as adults, but this is a mistake, especially strength/power exercises. It is generally recommended that pre-pubertal children should not lift heavy weights, although light exercises are unlikely to cause harm. Depending upon the child's development, thirteen or fourteen years is probably the best age at which to start a weight-training programme which should emphasise technique and skill learning under qualified supervision.

SPEED TRAINING

The soccer players who have conscientiously trained with resistance exercises (especially the power exercises such as the power clean, Fig 17 or plyometrics, Fig 26) should find that their overall movement speeds have improved. There are however, different types of speed in sport. The ability to react quickly to a stimulus is called reaction time and in soccer is illustrated by the reaction of the goalkeeper to the ball being kicked during a penalty. Reaction time here is the time between the stimulus, when he or she receives a signal that the ball is being kicked and the start of the movement. Reaction time can be improved with practice, but only so far; goalkeepers will never be able to react at the same split second as the ball is kicked.

Equally important in sport is the ability to react and move which is called response time. It is little help to react quickly mentally when the ball is being kicked, if you are slow moving to the ball. It is also important, in sprinting speed for example, to be able to maintain your speed – this is speed endurance. Sometimes, however, it is better to have controlled speed rather than flat-out speed which may create some technical problems. For example, it may be better to run just less than flat-out but then draw the opposition and give a well-timed pass rather than simply to run at full speed and not have the control needed to give a good pass.

Given the strength and power training already outlined, the soccer player is advised to combine this with speed and agility drills. Some examples of which are:

(i)   shuttle running across small sectors of the pitch;
(ii)   pressure drills requiring good response time (for example receiving and giving passes at speed);
(iii)   sprint drills.

Often response time can be improved simply through experience because the player has become more efficient at reading the game and so is more likely to be able to anticipate what will happen next.

Assessing Speed and Agility

Assessing sprint speed is relatively easy, although the validity of such measures will depend upon the accuracy of the timekeeper. Also, the distance used for sprint time-trials should be matched to the requirements of the players. The forty-metre sprint speed is often used as a measure of the type of speed needed in field team games such as football.

Agility is a desirable characteristic in soccer. An excellent means of testing agility is the Illinois agility run, shown in Fig 35. However, since this involves running for over fifteen

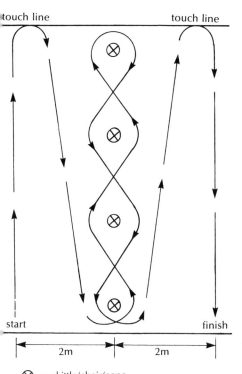

touch line   touch line

|← 2m →|← 2m →|

start   finish

⊗ = skittle/chair/cone
Note: start position is lying face down on the floor with hands by the shoulders and head on the start line.

Fig 35 Illinois agility run, reproduced with permission from Adams, J. et al., Foundations of Physical Activity (Stipes, 1965).

seconds, a shorter and more dynamic test might be more appropriate for soccer. An example of this test is given in Fig 36 – called the Nebraska agility test, it was originally designed for American footballers, but it provides a useful test for soccer players as well. Of course, there is no reason why soccer coaches should not devise their own agility test along similar lines.

FLEXIBILITY TRAINING

Flexibility is the most neglected area of sports fitness. Certainly this is the case for most sports; with the possible exceptions of gymnastics, swimming and some athletics events. Most games players are notoriously inflexible, especially footballers. Flexibility is important for the following reasons:

(i)   enhanced flexibility can help in the prevention and rehabilitation of injury;
(ii)   poor flexibility can inhibit the development of some skills;
(iii)   poor flexibility can reduce the effectiveness of other fitness parameters.

Flexibility therefore, is not just for dancers and gymnasts. Serious footballers do need good flexibility (which really means the range of movement at a joint or joint complex) and should be spending five to ten minutes a day doing stretching exercises.

Methods of Flexibility Training

There are three main forms of flexibility training: static flexibility, ballistic flexibility and PNF (proprioceptive neuromuscular facilitation).

Static Flexibility

This method involves stretching a muscle to the point of mild tension and then holding it for a length of time in the stretched position. This time may vary but should not be for less than ten seconds. Although some people suggest at least thirty seconds, this can be boring and may lead to players neglecting their flexibility training regardless of the fact that it has a beneficial physical effect.

Static stretching is a very effective means of improving flexibility and is recommended for all football players. It should always be performed prior to vigorous activity and before ballistic flexibility exercises. The best time to improve flexibility is when the muscles are warm, so an ideal time is after a game or training session. However, static stretching

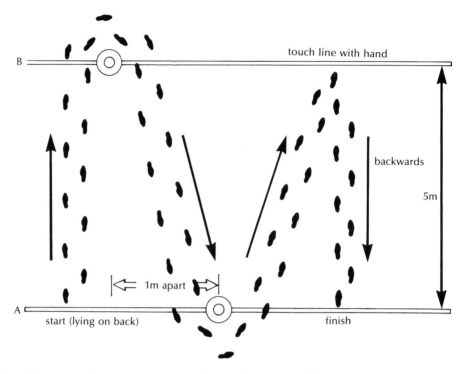

touch line with hand

backwards

5m

B

A

1m apart

start (lying on back)

finish

Fig 36   Nebraska agility test, reproduced with permission from Epley, B., The Strength of Nebraska (University of Nebraska, 1980).

stop here

Preparatory Stretch	Developmental Stretch	Forceful Over-stretch
as part of warm-up	to improve flexibility	too much
to prepare for activity	best done after vigorous exercise	don't

Fig 37   The stretch continuum.

should also be included as part of the warm-up (as mentioned at the beginning of this chapter). Fig 37 shows the stretch continuum. Players should not stretch in a drastic way in the belief that 'more must be better' but merely stretch to the point of mild tension rather than pain.

Partners can be used to help stretch a little further, but remember that the athlete stretching is in charge. This is particularly important when groups of children are performing flexibility exercises.

Ballistic Flexibility

A further type of flexibility is ballistic stretching. Here the muscles are stretched by using bouncing or bobbing movements at the end of the range. There has been some controversy over this type of stretching since it has been implicated as a cause of injury. However, while it should never be recommended for people on health-related exercise programmes (particularly older people or those with a history

68

f joint injury), it is a beneficial exercise for sportspeople because most sports require participants to stretch while moving. The most obvious example is the hurdler who performs ten ballistic stretches in each race. Ballistic stretching, therefore, *is* a necessary part of sport, but precautions must be taken to avoid injury. Such precautions should include a good warm-up, including static stretches, to prepare the body for more ballistic activity. Care should be taken that at the end of the range of motion the bouncing or bobbing is both controlled and gradual. These types of stretches should be specific to the movement required in soccer (for example high leg kicks).

PNF Flexibility

PNF is a more advanced and highly effective method of stretching. It involves three basic stages:

i)   contraction of the muscle to be stretched (for about ten seconds);
ii)   relaxation of the same muscle;
iii)   contraction of the antagonist (opposite) muscle or the use of partner assistance stretch the muscle.

The technique is believed to be effective because the initial muscular contraction allows the muscle to be stretched further. Most of the exercises shown can be adapted for PNF, but you should remember that the muscular contraction will not be effective without something to work against and so apparatus or partner resistance is required. You should use the static method when stretching during PNF (see Figs 38 and 39 for explanations of the flexibility exercises and also Figs 40–50).

Problem Flexibility Exercises

Not all flexibility exercises are necessarily good exercises. Because the muscles are being stretched, a strain is being put on the joints. In most cases, the joints, as well as ligaments and tendons, are being stretched in an acceptable way, but sometimes the joint can be twisted or put under pressure in such a way that the exercise is potentially harmful. Figs 51 and 52 show two of the most common flexibility exercises which should, as a general rule, be avoided.

The ballistic standing toe touch can lead to back problems and should never be performed by anyone who has experienced back trouble in the past. It is better for all athletes to use the sit and reach exercise in Fig 54. The hurdler stretch (Fig 52) may lead to problems for those with knee injuries and should therefore be avoided by footballers because, although this exercise can be effective in improving the flexibility of the hamstrings and groin, it puts a great deal of pressure on the knee joint.

Developing flexibility, like the other components of fitness, requires planning. Fig 53 summarises the FITT principle as it relates to flexibility training for soccer players.

Assessing Flexibility

Any of the flexibility exercises may be used as tests by simply recording measurements. However, two tests of flexibility are particularly recommended. The first is the sit and reach test which provides a good indication of flexibility in the hamstrings and lower back – an important part of the body in which to have good flexibility since it can help prevent lower back problems. This test is shown in Fig 54.

The second flexibility test is the lying shoulder lift test (Fig 55); it is particularly important for goalkeepers to have good shoulder flexibility. Another way to see whether your shoulder flexibility is symmetrical is to try the test in Fig 56. You will probably be better with one hand uppermost rather than the other, showing that shoulder flexibility is usually uneven; flexibility exercises are useful in remedying this.

69

Figure	Exercise	Muscles stretched	Starting position
40	Calf stretch	Calf	Lean against wall, foot pointing forwards.
41	Hamstring and lower back stretch	Hamstrings, lower back	Sit on floor, feet together and legs straight.
42	Hip stretch	Front of hip	Lunge position on floor.
43	Groin stretch	Groin, inside thighs	Sit on floor, legs folded with soles of feet together.
44	Side stretch	Side (oblique) abdominals	Upright stance, feet astride.
45	Shoulder stretch	Shoulders, chest	(i) Standing. (ii) Seated – leg in front.
46	Wrist stretch	Forearms	Kneeling on floor, hands flat.
47	Arm stretch	Shoulder, side of chest	Kneeling on all fours, arm out-stretched.
48	Lying stretch	(all-round stretch)	Lying face-up on floor.

Fig 38 Explanations of static flexibility exercises.

Figure	Exercise	Muscles stretched	Starting position	Movement	Other points
49	PNF hamstring stretch	Hamstrings	Sitting on floor, feet together and legs straight.	Contraction: push against partner and push down into the ground with both legs (10 secs), then relax. Stretch: reach forwards (with or without partner assistance) towards toes.	
50	PNF shoulder stretch	Shoulder, chest	Sitting or kneeling, arms out-stretched to the side, parallel with floor.	Contraction: pull arms forwards against partner resistance (10secs), then relax. Stretch: partner pulls arms back, keeping them parallel to the floor.	Can also be done with arms above head.

Fig 39   Explanations of PNF flexibility exercises.

Movement	Other points
(i) To stretch outer calf, keep leg straight and push heel into ground. Push hips forwards. (ii) To stretch inner calf (soleus), bend leg and push forwards and downwards with hip. Keep heel on ground.	Vary position of toes.
Sit up first (chest out) then stretch forwards to the toes.	Vary leg positions (apart).
Push hips forwards.	Progress to more upright trunk position with rear foot on toes.
Gently ease knees outwards and downwards.	Use pressure from arms if necessary.
Bend sideways and hold position.	Avoid leaning forwards.
Lift arms upwards and backwards. Partner lifts arms upwards and backwards, or sideways.	(iii) If partner places a knee in the back of the exerciser, this can help stability.
Fingers pointing towards the body, pull shoulders back to stretch forearms.	Change direction of fingers.
Pull shoulder back to produce stretch on top of shoulder, arm and side of chest.	Reach out with hand first.
Extend body position as much as possible.	

Fig 40   Calf stretch.

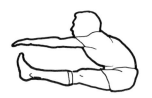

Fig 41   Hamstring and lower back stretch.

Fig 42   Hip stretch.

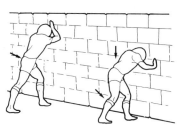

Fig 43   Groin stretch.

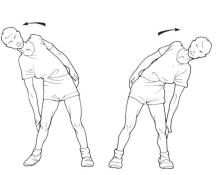

Fig 44   Side stretch.

Fig 45   Shoulder stretch.

Fig 46   Wrist stretch.

Fig 47   Arm stretch.

Fig 48   Lying stretch.

Fig 49   PNF hamstring stretch.

Fig 50   PNF shoulder stretch.

Fig 51   Ballistic standing toe touch.

Fit 52   Hurdler stretch.

FITT Component	Suggested guidelines
Frequency	Can be done every day once some experience has been gained. Initially, every other day.
Intensity	To point of mild tension in the stretched muscle.
Time	Each exercise 10–30secs. Each session 5–15mins.
Type (of exercise)	Static stretches, followed by PNF and ballistic. Progress from preparatory to developmental stretching.

Fig 53   FITT principle for flexibility exercises.

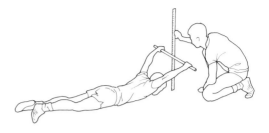

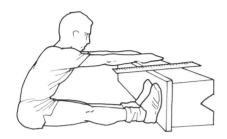

Fig 54   Sit and reach flexibility test.

Fig 55   Lying shoulder reach test.

Fig 56   Behind back shoulder flexibility test.

CHAPTER COOL-DOWN

After covering the main aspects of physical fitness for soccer, it is appropriate to cool down before moving on to the next chapter.

This cool-down is a summary of the main points:

(i)   physical fitness is multi-dimensional. The main components requiring physical training are: cardiorespiratory fitness (stamina), muscular endurance, strength and power, speed and flexibility;

(ii)   proper planning of fitness training must take into account the frequency, intensity, time and type of exercises (FITT principle), as well as specificity and reversibility;

(iii)   soccer players should always warm up and cool down before and after a match or a training session;

(iv)   nearly all footballers require high levels of aerobic fitness, but should also be well trained in strength, power, speed and muscular endurance;

(v)   flexibility has often been a particularly neglected aspect of soccer training but is an important component of fitness.

THE HENLEY COLLEGE LIBRARY

3 Healthy Eating

Players must be well-prepared physically on the day of the match. Their preparation has involved many training sessions over the previous months or years. Food has been providing the energy for the players to maintain the body and to train. Nutrients in the food – protein, vitamins and minerals – have been used to replenish body losses incurred on a day to day basis. Food is crucial for the training process.

Food can also be important on psychological and social levels. It may be psychologically important to eat favourite foods or those believed to help performance. For this reason (and probably this reason alone) these foods (often highly peculiar to an individual) are eaten to ensure that peak performance is reached and maintained. We all enjoy eating out with a group of friends and do not want to appear too odd by choosing unusual foods. On social occasions players may therefore choose foods which they know are unsuitable. If this happens on an occasional basis it does not matter, but if it is a regular occurrence then it is important to ask why this is the case. It must be emphasised that performance on the day depends primarily on the long period of preceding training and this includes the diet.

Eating for your sport can be broken down into two subdivisions; eating for training (which also means for good health) and eating for matches. Both are influenced by who we are, where we are and the company we keep.

REQUIREMENTS FOR FOOD

Eating and drinking is taken for granted by most people. We eat and drink without too much thought and assume that our bodily needs will be met and indeed most of the time they will. However, whether these needs are being met optimally is the question that all serious sportspeople should address.

The human body is marvellously resilient, tolerant and versatile. If food-energy intake is less than the body needs, the body conserves energy in order to 'balance the books'. People on reducing diets have been observed to be less active and physically slower (so conserving energy) than before embarking on their diet. This has implications for the athlete who is training and deliberately reducing food intake. If the fuel supply is limited in this way the level of effort put into the player's training can only be lowered. For when fed less than they need, young children become less active and grow less quickly as their bodies attempt to balance their 'energy books'. If a young player is exercising hard and not able to eat a sufficient amount, it is likely that growth and/or the rate of exercise will suffer. It is not possible to get energy out if insufficient food is consumed.

However, there comes a point when the body can no longer adapt to an insufficient intake of food-energy and at this point functions begin to deteriorate very noticeably. Body tissues are not repaired efficiently – they may be broken down and not replaced at all, levels of activity become very noticeably poor and general health deteriorates with increased likelihood of infection. Professional medical investigation and treatment may then be essential.

The body thus has an adaptive capability and a deficiency response. At the other end of the spectrum (and much more likely to occur in western countries) the body reacts to excessive food-energy intake. Food consumption above requirement will not raise the level of activity or turn individuals into super-performers, although it will encourage rapid growth – in children upwards, and in adults outwards. Eating more protein than the body needs or can use, simply results in the excess being excreted. The same is true of water-soluble vitamins such as vitamin C and some minerals such as sodium chloride (salt). In the case of fat-soluble vitamins such as vitamin A, and certain minerals such as iron which the body cannot so easily dispose of, excess stores can ultimately be life-threatening. Players, therefore, need to take special care with regard to the dangers of over-indulgence, especially when it comes to diet supplements. Regular monitoring of body weight can provide information about meeting nutrient requirements or meeting them in excess.

Indeed there is the *Recommended Amounts of Food Energy and Nutrients for Groups of People in the UK* (DHSS, 1979) which provides a useful guide. There is no evidence that sportspeople need any more nutrients than non-sportspeople, providing that they are eating a good variety of foods which will meet their energy needs. These needs may well vary from season to season and during different training periods. The total amount of food consumed may therefore also vary.

In summary, the overall needs of the player in training will be both unique and in that athlete variable. This variation may be masked by the ability of the individual to adapt to different levels of nutrition, but it is essential that such adaptation is not allowed to mask impending deficiency. Players and their coaches must remain vigilant.

WHAT'S IN FOOD?

Food is a mixture of nutrients; fat, carbohydrate, protein, vitamins and minerals. Everyone needs these nutrients in the same way. Eating food ultimately enables these nutrients to be made available to our bodies. All naturally occurring foods contain all nutrients, but in differing amounts (dependent upon the function which it performed in the source plant or animal). For example, leaves are not storage organs and so their energy content is low. Meat, however, is largely muscle and so has a high protein content.

In Fig 57 there is a list of foods and some of the nutrients they contain. A more comprehensive list is given in the *Manual of Nutrition* (HMSO, 1985).

Sources of Carbohydrate
(Milk and milk products also provide significant amounts of calcium).

1 glass of milk — Supplies about 8g protein, 12g CHO, 8g fat, 150kcals.

For reduced energy and fat:
1 glass of skimmed milk or 1 carton plain yoghurt — Supplies about 8g protein, 12g CHO, 80kcals.

Cereals and legumes – high carbohydrate and some protein.
1 thin/medium slice white bread*
½ roll, bun, crumpet, teacake etc.
1 tbs white flour*
1 digestive biscuit
   (also contains one portion of fat)
4 tbs unsweetened breakfast cereal*
3 tbs baked beans* or other cooked
   bean*/pea*/lentil*
   (also contains one third of portion of
   'meat' protein)
3–4 tbs fresh/processed peas
1 tbs apple crumble/pie
   (also contains one portion of fat and
   one 'fruit' carbohydrate portion)

Each portion supplies about 2g protein, 15g CHO as starch and 70kcals.

Fruit and vegetables – also supply important vitamins.
Small apple, pear, orange
½ small banana
10–12 cherries or grapes
2 medium plums, prunes, apricots,
   dates (dried)
1 tbs raisins, currants
2 tbs any vegetable (except avocado –
   add four portions of fat)
1 small/medium potato, boiled or baked
   (if fried add one portion of fat)

Each portion supplies about 0–2g protein, 5–10g CHO as sugars and 25–40kcals.

Sources of Fat
Small scrap butter or margarine (5g)
1 tsp oil
2 tsp mayonnaise
1 slice fried streaky bacon
5 olives
10 roasted peanuts
2 tsp double cream

Each portion supplies about 5g fat, 45kcals.

Sources of Protein
Meat and fish – also rich sources of minerals and vitamins.

60–85g cooked (not fried) meat* or oily fish
60g hard cheese
85g edam, gouda, brie or similar
3 grilled sausages (add one portion of fat)

Each portion supplies about 20–25g protein, 15–20g fat, 200–250kcals.

For reduced energy and fat:
60–85g cooked chicken (no skin), veal or rabbit
60–85g cooked liver*
60–85g white fish
60–85g tuna in brine or 4 pilchards
170g cottage cheese

Each portion supplies about 20–25g protein, 5g fat, 150kcals, but do not fry or add fat.

Sources of Thiamin or Vitamin B1
Milk and milk products — all milk and soya milk

Cereals and legumes — all legumes**, fortified (non-wholemeal) bread**, flour products and fortified breakfast cereals

Meat and fish — ham and pork products, liver
Fruit and vegetables — none
Other — brewers' yeast

Sources of Riboflavin or Vitamin B2
Milk and milk products — all types of milk**
Cereals and legumes — only fortified breakfast cereals
Meat and fish — liver
Fruit and vegetables — dark-green leafed vegetables
Other — brewers' yeast

Sources of Pyridoxine or Vitamin B6
Milk and milk products — none
Cereals and legumes — all legumes**
Meat and fish — beef, pork, lamb, tuna and salmon
Fruit and vegetables — bananas and potatoes
Other — nuts

Sources of Calcium
Milk and milk products — all milk**, cheese**, yoghurt
Cereals and legumes — fortified flour and products (not wholemeal), tofu

Meat and fish	salmon and sardines if bones consumed
Fruit and vegetables	dark-green leafed vegetables
Other	molasses and unhulled sesame seeds (as in tahini)

Sources of Iron

Milk and milk products	none
Cereals and legumes	fortified flour and products**, fortified breakfast cereals, all legumes**
Meat and fish	red meats**, liver**
Fruit and vegetables	dark-green leafed vegetables
Other	molasses, chocolate and cocoa

Sources of Zinc

Milk and milk products	cheese
Cereals and legumes	all legumes, bread, wholemeal flour and products
Meat and fish	meat**, liver, crab and shellfish
Fruit and vegetables	very small amounts in most fruit and vegetables
Other	nuts

*   also rich in iron
** particularly rich source

Fig 57   Nutrients contained in typical portions of food.

THE NEED FOR FLUID, ENERGY AND NUTRIENTS

Fluid

Our bodies are about seventy per cent water, so in a 70kg person 49kg is water. Cells (the constituents of every living thing) and blood need water in order to dissove and carry nutrients. Even a slight reduction in body water of two to five per cent (1.5–3.5l or 3–6pts) can cause a reduced efficiency in cellular function. Dehydration also does not allow the body sufficient water to cool itself and so the body may overheat. This makes us feel disorientated and undoubtedly reduces performance. Fluid balance or hydration must therefore be of prime importance to all sportspeople, including footballers. Water is normally lost in three ways:

(i)   through the urine. This volume is increased by taking more water or by certain nutrients such as alcohol (which has a diuretic effect);

(ii)   through the skin. This normally accounts for a small percentage, but during exercise can rise to over three litres per hour, depending on the intensity of exercise and the environmental conditions;
(iii)   through the lungs.

Water can also be lost abnormally in two ways:

(i)   through diarrhoea. This may be caused by infection or by eating too much fibre or simple carbohydrate, which cannot be absorbed; they also cause water to be drawn into the gut from the body tissues (causing cell dehydration);
(ii)   through fevers. Extra water is lost through the skin in order to reduce body temperature.

Clearly it is important to avoid extra fluid loss and this means taking care not to consume foods of dubious origin (including ice cubes when abroad) and choosing carbohydrate foods wisely (see later in this chapter).

Replacing the fluid lost during training sessions and matches is vital. Our normal thirst 'mechanisms' may not operate successfully at this level of loss and are therefore unreliable. Water loss needs to be actively monitored, which means weighing yourself before and after any exercise. The change in weight will reflect the loss of body water which must then be replaced. The best way to do this is to use a drink which is 'isotonic' to body fluids (the same concentration) or 'hypotonic' (weaker concentration). Drinks that are 'hyper-tonic' (more concentrated than body fluid) may cause fluid to be drawn into the gut to dilute it and should therefore be avoided as it will cause (osmotic) diarrhoea. However, there are some fluids commercially available which minimize this effect. To be on the safe side it is found that the following solution served cold, as from the fridge, in about half pint quantities is ideal: 2.5g of sugar per 100 ml (about ½oz per pint), 23mg of sodium (1.0 mmol) per 100 ml (a very small pinch per pint), 20mg of potassium (0.5 mmol) per 100 ml (a smaller pinch per pint). Fortunately a dilute solution of orange squash (two – three tablespoons per pint) is just about the correct concentration. If using a commercially prepared drink, it is wise to check the concentration, which should not be greater than those given above. Do not leave this sort of experimentation until game or match time, try the drink during a hard training session. Plain water is also a perfect replacement fluid. Whatever is chosen it is important to consume a replacement amount. Two pints weighs about 1 kg (2lb) and is equivalent to about one litre; it takes some practice and training to consume the quantities required. Caffeine in foods and drinks is a diuretic and will cause extra fluid loss. A drink which contains alcohol causes extra urinary loss of water too (it is a strong diuretic). Pints of beer will not do.

Finally before matches, players can prepare for the fluid which is to be lost. By carefully monitoring losses during training it is possible to make some predictions and so consume some fluid to cover anticipated losses – but take care not to include a sugar source. Fluid (with an energy source) intake at half-time may be crucial to how the game ends. It should not be necessary to take extra food energy at half time, unless to satisfy psychological demands. The energy stored in the body should be more than sufficient.

Requirements for Energy and Nutrients

The nutritional requirements of each player will depend on several factors, including age, sex and body-weight (growing children or teenagers need proportionally greater amounts of food than adults, women need more iron than men and men need more energy because they often weigh more) and duration and intensity of exercise.

The above list is particularly true when considering the amount of energy required. It is less applicable with regard to the need for protein, minerals and vitamins.

ENERGY

Energy is derived from fat and carbohydrate (CHO) in food and, to a lesser extent, protein. The amount of energy in food is measured in units corresponding to the amount of heat that food would produce when it is 'burned' in the body. The heat produced can be thought of as providing the power to make the body work in much the same way as a coal fire produces heat to make steam to turn an engine. These units of 'heat' are calories.

A calorie is a very tiny amount of heat and the amount in food is thousands of calories or kilocalories (kcals). Another unit which is used to measure the amount of energy in food is the joule – again a very tiny unit of 'work-energy' and so expressed in kilojoules (kJ). One kilocalorie is equivalent to 4.2 kilojoules (1kcal = 4.2kJ). Large amounts of kilojoules are expressed as megajoules (MJ), that is 1000kJ to a megajoule.

Energy in the food is used to do 'internal work'; it keeps the heart beating and the lungs and other organs working, even when we are asleep. This basic, essential requirement for energy is known as the basal metabolic rate (BMR) and varies with body size. BMR has the first priority for energy, however much food is ingested. The other basic needs for energy are the renewal of body tissues and the excretion of waste products. After these energy requirements have been met, dietary energy is used for 'external' work. The amount of external work performed can be moderated to fit the dietary energy supply. The energy devoted to the synthesis of new tissue can also be moderated. The extra energy required for the synthesis of 1kg (2lbs) of new tissue has been estimated to be as high as 5000 to 7000 kcals (about 21 to 29.4 MJ) above normal dietary intake.

SOURCES OF ENERGY

Carbohydrates as Dietary Sources of Energy

Plants store their energy as carbohydrate (CHO). This is a term used to cover a variety of molecules which all have similar chemical properties. Some molecules are small, taste sweet and are known as simple, or sugary, carbohydrate. They include glucose, sucrose (sugar), fructose, maltose and lactose (although lactose is an anomaly since mammals produce it in milk for their young). Some molecules are large, do not taste sweet and are called complex, or starchy, carbohydrate (the starches in bread, potatoes, rice and pasta are all complex). Finally, there are some forms of carbohydrate which we cannot digest or absorb and which are known as unavailable carbohydrate or dietary fibre. Eventually *all* dietary sources of the sugary and starchy carbohydrate, (available CHO) will be transformed into glucose in the blood.

Each gram of available CHO provides 4kcals of energy to the body. It is found in all foods of plant origin: cereals, fruit, vegetables (including pulses such as dried peas, beans and lentils) and to a limited extent in nuts (*see* Fig 57). Fruit and vegetables contain a very high percentage of water and so the carbohydrate which is present is considerably diluted. For this reason these foods are less 'energy-dense', which also applies to other nutrients which are similarly diluted. It also means that to consume a large amount of energy a great quantity of these foods needs to be eaten. This is useful for slimmers, but not necessarily for the person who requires a high energy intake in a hurry. However, foods made from cereal grains (bread, pasta and biscuits or cakes and so on) do not contain as much water and so are more energy-dense. Bread, breakfast cereals, pasta and rice are all rich sources of CHO and are relatively energy-dense.

Once the CHO is consumed it appears in the blood as glucose. This can be used directly for energy or stored in the muscle or in the liver as glycogen, the 'animal equivalent' of starch – a very important source of energy for all animal cells. There is a finite amount of glycogen which can be stored, about 200g (7 oz). The glycogen stored in the muscle probably determines the amount of work which can be done by that muscle. Any excess glucose is then made into fat and stored in the adipose tissue.

Fats as Dietary Sources of Energy

Fat is found in almost all foods, since it is an important part of the cell wall of all plant and animal tissue. Plants do not store energy as fat (except in nuts) so the amount of fat in plant sources of food will be very low. Animals, including humans, store energy in their bodies as fat; indeed an average man may have 14 kg (30 lbs) of fat in his body. This fat is stored in many places; in adipose tissue around vital organs, under the skin and amongst muscle fibres. Meat (muscle tissue) and animal products such as eggs, milk and milk products all contain fat, often in significant amounts (*see* Fig 57).

Fat is energy-dense and supplies 9 kcals per gram, more than twice as much per unit weight as CHO. Animal products do not contain as much water as fruit and vegetables and so are much more energy- and nutrient-dense. Fat can also taste nice; think of the taste of fried mushrooms compared to boiled or the taste of buttered rather than dry toast. Eating fat is easy and because it is energy-dense it provides energy in small amounts of food; hence over-indulgence is easy. Active and busy athletes need this form of energy which can be eaten in a hurry, but people trying to lose weight need to be careful.

Sources of Energy in the Diet and Long-Term Health

The amount and type of food-energy we consume may influence our health. It is generally agreed that there is a weight–height ratio at which adults are fitter and less prone to developing various life-threatening diseases. The more fat you carry, the higher will be the ratio and the higher the risk of such diseases occuring. A simple way to calculate whether your weight–height ratio is satisfactory is to use this internationally-accepted method: weight (kg) divided by height (metres), squared. This is termed the body mass index (or BMI). The range thought to be acceptable is 17–25. If your BMI is below the bottom end, this is just as disturbing as being above the top number. For if weight is reduced too far it leads to poor body reserves of nutrients due to the restrictive dietary intake. A very restrictive intake can lead to nutrient deficiencies which will ultimately affect performance.

This weight – height ratio (BMI) is a simple and quick test. However, it does not tell us exactly how much of an individual is fat and how much is lean (muscle) tissue. To find out the ratio of fat to lean tissue a more specific measurement has to be made. One method which can be used is based on the assumption that the fat under the skin is a fair reflection of total body fat. Using special, skinfold callipers (*see* Fig 58) the amount of fat under the skin can be assessed. The total body fat can then be estimated by using a formula (Eisenman and Johnson, 1982). Women, for physiological reasons, have a higher percentage body fat than men. The amount of fat which different people have varies and can be manipulated by use of exercise and diet, although the difference between men and women always remains. A list of measured body fats is given below:

Average adult male (20–50 years)	15–25 per cent fat
Average adult female (20–50 years)	26–35 per cent fat
Adult male (distance) runner	6–13 per cent fat
Adult female (distance) runner	15–19 per cent fat
Adult male soccer player	about 19 per cent fat
Adult female soccer player	about 23 per cent fat

The type of 'energy' consumed may have an effect on long-term health. It is thought advisable to consume the majority of energy in the form of carbo-

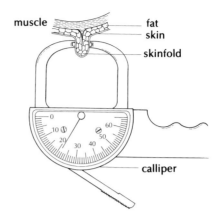

Fig 58   Estimating body fat with skinfold callipers.

hydrate. Sugary carbohydrate can cause dental disease and therefore reliance should be on the complex, or starchy, carbohydrate. Fat is thought to be associated with heart disease and certain forms of cancer and for these reasons it is best avoided in large amounts. The saturated fats found in animal sources are thought to be more harmful than the fats from vegetable sources, which are largely unsaturated.

The development of certain diseases which mainly afflict people in the developed countries are probably due to a number of factors, two of these are diet and lack of exercise. At this time it is difficult to say how 'protective' exercise, if practised intensively, will be in the long term. Certainly it is important for soccer players to meet energy and food needs, which may mean eating more fat than would normally be advised for the general public. But it is not known what the effects on long-term health will be.

PROTEIN

The requirement for dietary protein depends on several factors including: the amount of muscle tissue present (the more muscle tissue, the more body protein there is to maintain and replace); the amount of new tissue synthesis (in the growth phase proportionally more protein is required and also there is increased demand for energy for synthesis of this into new tissue); the amount lost through sweat and hair/skin loss.

Much controversy surrounds the nature and extent of the body's needs for protein. The body can become very efficient at conserving its store of protein which is found in every cell in the body. It would seem that soccer players need the same amount of protein per kilogram of body-weight as untrained individuals, although they will need more if energy supplies are not sufficient to meet demand, since protein can be broken down and used in the same way as glucose to provide the body with energy. This, however, is very wasteful because once it is used for energy, it cannot be used for body protein 'repair'.

It is not surprising, therefore, that there is a close relationship between protein and energy requirements; if enough carbohydrate and fat are consumed, requirements for energy are met and protein does not need to be used. All the protein consumed can be used for tissue repair and body maintenance. In which case the protein requirements for players will be no greater than for anyone else. Supplementary proteins are often used by sporting people, but unlike the protein in food, commercially sold supplements do not usually contain a supply of energy – which means that they will not be well used. Work currently in progress at Leeds Polytechnic tends to indicate that the consumption of protein supplements can actually cause some athletes to reduce their overall food intake. This is clearly counter-productive in terms of maintaining an adequate energy and nutrient supply. Finally, it should be stated that protein will *only* be incorporated into muscle tissue if there is an appropriate training programme.

Amino acids are the tiny molecules which are joined together in particular sequences to make proteins. Proteins in hair will have a different sequence to the proteins in muscle (which is why hair and muscle look so different). Once again, all proteins contain all amino acids but in different amounts, depending on source and function. Generally proteins from animal sources are nearer in amino acid pattern and proportion to our own bodies and our needs. However, it is possible to get all amino acids from plant sources. Vegetarians do this and are perfectly healthy. It is quite possible to rely on the cheaper vegetable sources of protein and, by mixing foods together, a better mix of amino acids is ensured. Putting cereals (bread, pasta, rice) together with nuts or pulses (dried beans, peas or lentils) creates a perfect complement of amino acids precisely the same as that found in the best sirloin steak.

How Much Protein?

The actual amount of protein needed per person is difficult to define. It is possible to give values for grams of protein, but this is meaningless unless it is put into the context of food. Values for adults of between 1–2g of protein per kg of body-weight per day have been quoted. For someone who weighs 80 kg the need for protein could be estimated at 80–160g per day. The values given in the Department of Health and Social Security's recommended intake tables are comparable to this. About 40 kcals of energy are required per gram of protein. In the above example this would mean a food energy intake of between 3,200 and 6,400 kcals per day.

Food, however, is a mixture of nutrients and if the food in the diet provides, say, 3,000 kcals, then this amount is likely to contain at least 80g of protein or probably a lot more. It is very difficult to consume too little protein when eating a variety of foods (*see* Fig 57 which shows some sources of protein).

Making Weight

Consuming more protein than you actually need is now seen as counter-productive. The only way of actually gaining weight is to follow a rigorous and intensive exercise programme which increases the muscle tissue. The energy required to sustain this level of exercise is considerable and one suspects that if muscle is not being laid down it is because the intensity of the exercise is inadequate. Muscular activity needs energy, which is derived from food and stored as either glycogen or fat. Glycogen is often limited in supply and so is probably the major constraint on duration and intensity of exercise. The amount of food consumed should be sufficient to cover both energy and protein needs, but if the food consumed contains high amounts of fat and protein then the dietary energy presented to the body is lacking in carbohydrate. This deficiency means that little glycogen will be stored and if the amount of glycogen stored determines the intensity and duration of the training then it follows that to make weight the diet should be high in carbohydrate (*see* Fig 57). So to increase your muscular strength you need to eat plenty of CHO foods like bread and potatoes rather than protein.

MINERALS AND VITAMINS

There is also little evidence to suggest that athletes have a greater bodily demand for vitamins compared to non-athletes. As has been said, food is a mixture of nutrients and as food intake rises (as it must do to support activity) then so does the level of vitamin supply through the food. A very bizarre diet indeed would have to be chosen for any deficiency to occur. However, it is possible to over-indulge in vitamin supplements – this can be dangerous. It is becoming apparent that not only can over-indulging in vitamins (even vitamin C) lead to the development of harmful conditions, but also that such supplements affect the absorption of other nutrients. If supplements are thought to be necessary medical advice should first be sought to confirm a positive need.

Minerals may be thought of in two groups, those which we require in relatively large amounts and those which we require in trace amounts. The former which are of importance here are sodium, potassium and calcium. Of those required in very small amounts the most important is iron. Sodium and potassium loss in sweat barely reaches levels whereby supplements are required above normal dietary intake and therefore they should not be considered outside the context of a normal varied diet.

There is, however, perhaps slightly more concern over adequate iron intake in athletes, due to the occasional occurrence of the condition known as 'sports anaemia' although it has not been ascribed to soccer players. The reason for this anaemia is not fully understood but may be a result of physical stress on the red blood cells or from abnormal losses of blood – both due to the intensity and prolonged effort of training and exercise. If anaemia is diagnosed then iron supplements will need to be taken. It would also be wise to make sure the diet contains iron-rich foods (*see* Fig 57).

Overall, the athlete who is not restricting intake should not need any vitamin or mineral supplements. In any event supplements should only be commenced after a deficiency has been confirmed through medical testing.

TRAINING SCHEDULES AND FOOD FOR MATCHES

Rest periods are a vital part of successful training and allow the player to replenish energy (especially glycogen) and nutrient stores. Any schedule must, of course, allow time for the preparation and consumption of food. Obviously, without food we simply do not have the energy available to perform and it must therefore be an essential part of the training schedule. Indeed it may well be that relaxation periods should become eating periods. 'Tapering' of exercise before a match allows for just this repletion phase. Productivity of training might well be improved if coaches and players were to give more thought to rest and food periods.

Timing of meals should be arranged so that the major part of digestion is complete before activity commences. Fat and protein foods on the whole, take longer to move through the stomach and small intestine (2–4 hours). Carbohydrate and cold foods are much quicker (1–2 hours, depending upon the size of the meal). Players need to eat after a training session and good anticipation of food needs is essential. As it may not always be possible to consume a full meal, it is sensible to take your own food (i.e. some sandwiches and a flask of fluid to provide the essential nutrient and fluid replacement). If you do have to eat out then carbohydrate in the form of baked potatoes, pizza or pasta makes the most sensible foods. Meals and snacks should always be based on the starchy carbohydrates, since they are more effective at repleting glycogen stores lost during games and training sessions.

TRAINING FOR SOCCER

Training for soccer, primarily a sport performed under aerobic conditions, mainly aims to enhance the cardiovascular system and muscle. This ensures efficient and continuous supply of 'fuel' and oxygen to the working muscles for a long period. Training sessions at sub-maximal work load – aerobic training – also conditions the body to use its fat stores as the major fuel. This is important, especially under match conditions as the store of fat in the body is much greater than CHO and will therefore last for longer. However, fat is not the sole fuel and some CHO must also be used; this usage becomes proportionally greater as the intensity of the exercise increases – usually towards the end of a match or training session. It is the reserve of stored CHO present at this time that will determine the duration of intense work. For training sessions that are longer than an hour the amount of stored CHO (glycogen) determines the intensity of the work that the muscles can do. Power becomes increasingly difficult to generate in muscles that have diminishing amounts of available glycogen.

Soccer players do not only need stamina to see them through a hard match but also the strength for 'explosive' bursts of energy. These bursts demand an anaerobic metabolism when the only fuel source is glucose (glycogen). Training sessions therefore aim both to build muscles and to train them to work and tolerate anaerobic conditions. To achieve this exercises are normally carried out to exhaustion; this conditions the muscles to anaerobic metabolism and by its nature depletes glycogen quite quickly and thoroughly.

Training also seems to cause a change in the efficiency with which muscles store glycogen; it has been observed that training brings about swift, efficient repletion of stores, but only if muscles have a plentiful dietary supply. Generally, however, starchy carbohydrate may well be better at replacing the lost glycogen than sugary foods in the long term. It normally takes between twenty-four and forty-eight hours to replace glycogen supplies.

Aerobic conditioning means long training sessions which are also expensive in terms of energy usage; it is therefore essential to take time to eat properly during this training. Concentrated sources of CHO are important (*see* Fig 57) as well as high energy foods (containing fat) such as chocolate, rich cakes, nuts and biscuits. Drinks or soups are also useful, especially those using milk and adding sugar or cream. Nor should you forget to replace the fluids which will have been lost in vigorous training.

Soccer players may also need to consider their lean–fat ratio. The consideration of carrying excess body fat is an important part of training but it is vital that the level of body fat is steadily maintained. Constant dieting does little to afford you energy for effective training.

The Big Match

As match time approaches, the will to win must be combined with the suggested training programme. Diet can have a role to play in this, but food eaten immediately before a match has little effect of performance; it can in fact be detrimental. It is rather the extended period of preparation, training and diet which will affect performance on the day. Unlike food, however, it is imperative to drink before a match since lack of fluids – dehydration – may prevent you even finishing the ninety minutes.

How to Arrive Ready to Compete

The message of this chapter has been to ensure that you get the 'energy books balanced', which means ensuring that energy is replaced in the working muscle. If this becomes part of the training schedule then relaxing before the event and allowing the body muscles to recoup their energy reserves takes place quite naturally; that is to say you should 'taper' the training schedule.

In fact, it can be unproductive to follow an unusually high carbohydrate diet for several days before the event, as this can lead to discomfort and diarrhoea. By careful measurement of a player's food intake it has been shown how very difficult it is for the individual actually to judge by how much food intake is increasing. More often than not CHO intake is raised but the contribution to energy intake from fat is lowered, so the player is unable to achieve a sufficiently high overall energy intake. This means that instead of the carbohydrate being stored, it may be used for the essential work of body maintenance (so that glycogen storage is less than expected). The message here is that good dietary habits should develop and support training. This will also be highly suitable for immediate preparation for a match (which is often of shorter duration than the training sessions).

The planning of meals and snacks before a match also needs consideration. As already mentioned it is vital to have the intestine as free as possible from the process of digestion; meals should therefore be finished at least two hours (preferably four hours) before kick-off, since the anticipation of competition may reduce intestinal function. Players should carefully plan those meals which they feel will be most beneficial although the content of the meals is largely irrelevant in terms of providing energy which should have been stored over the past twelve to forty-eight hours. However, sugary snacks should be avoided as these may delay the release of internal energy (see below). It would also be wise to avoid those foods which are known to produce flatulence as this can be very uncomfortable during a match.

There are two factors which affect the utilisation of fuel. Firstly, taking something sugary about forty-five minutes before starting an event will 'catch the body out'; the body will be expecting to store food or nutrients and not to mobilise fuel. Moreover, the hormones which act to control body chemistry will not promote energy release, which can be very unfortunate for someone about to start a match. Secondly, the type of training will have determined how the player responds to the demands of the exercise; whether or not fat is predominantly 'burned ', so sparing glycogen.

Some ergogenic (or exercise-enhancing) aids may be tried. One which has some use, provided it is not misused by over-indulgence, is caffeine. Consumed about forty-five minutes before exercise it has two effects: it is a stimulant and reduces the subjective feeling of effort and it causes fatty acids to be 'mobilised' and used as fuel, so sparing glycogen.

The amount of caffeine which has been found to produce this effect is 4mg per kg of body-weight. Caffeine is found in chocolate to a small extent and in drinks in the following amounts:

1 cup (200ml) cola		35mg
1 cup (150ml) coffee,	instant	70mg
	percolated	120mg
	filter	160mg
1 cup (150ml) tea		50mg

Caffeine is a drug. If it is given in large and uncontrolled amounts it can produce vascular changes which are harmful. In addition, at everyday doses it can have a pronounced diuretic effect which is undesirable when hydration is required.

Indeed hydration is probably the single most important factor for success on the day. It is essential that fluid is replaced as often as possible during the match (but this is restricted to half-time). The concept of fluid with a suitable concentration, to ensure maximum absorption, has been discussed earlier.

Remember it is counter-productive to include glucose in the solution – the energy should already be stored in the muscles.

It is now suggested that taking a form of carbohydrate, after exercise has started, can prove beneficial. As CHO is absorbed and the glucose reaches the bloodstream it can be used by the working muscles. But two things need to be borne in mind. The time from swallowing the carbohydrate to it reaching the bloodstream is about thirty minutes. It is pointless taking the CHO some ten to fifteen minutes before the end of the game. Secondly, the CHO will only be absorbed if the exercise intensity is well within the aerobic capacity of the individual. The other consideration is the form it is best to take the CHO in. Solid food may take longer to empty from the stomach so it would seem sensible to take the CHO in the form of a drink, thereby replacing fluid and energy at the same time. A ten per cent solution of CHO is suggested as optimal – this would mean two level tablespoons of sugar in a pint of water. Whenever you try new drink solutions it is essential that it is not during a crucial match; the time for experimentation is during a training session.

Summary

The supply of energy and nutrients is crucial to sustain the desired level of exercise and performance. Training is recognised as making an important contribution to the performance of any serious soccer player. The fuel to support that level of exercise should not be left to chance nor should the overall health of the body. Food and its nutrients are therefore as important to consider as the player's exercise programme. The monitoring of food and fluid intake, as well as body-weight, should be part of the player's routine.

THE HENLEY COLLEGE LIBRARY

4   Injury Prevention

CLASSIFICATION OF INJURY

In order to prevent injuries it is preferable to understand why they occur and where they occur in the body. An injury may be due to an external force (extrinsic injury) or to a force within the body (intrinsic injury). Extrinsic injuries happen when a player collides with an object such as the goal-posts, the ground, a piece of equipment, or even another player. They can also be caused by an object hitting the body such as the ball. Intrinsic injuries may happen without any particular cause (incidental injury) but are more likely to occur when the training load is rapidly increased in intensity and frequency (overuse injury). Most injuries tend to occur quite suddenly (acute injury) but fortunately tend to settle very quickly. However, an acute injury may progress and become a chronic injury – these are usually more difficult to treat and take longer to overcome. You are far more likely to get injured towards the end of a training session or match, when you become tired, than at any other time, so take more care as you become fatigued.

SITE OF INJURY

Sports injuries may occur anywhere in the body such as in muscles, tendons (pullies attached to the bone from the muscles), tenosynovia (the protective sheaths around a tendon), ligaments (fibrous bands joining two bones together at a joint), joints and bones. It is helpful to grade the injuries into three groups:

(i)   Group A.   Minimal damage when only bruising occurs and there is no major disruption to the muscle, tendon, ligament or whatever. Small blood vessels are damaged, however, and leak blood which forms a bruise (haematoma).
(ii)   Group B.   Some disruption of the tissues takes place and a sprain, strain, partial tear or partial rupture takes place in a muscle, tendon (tendonitis), tendon sheath (tenosynovitis), ligament or bone (stress fracture). Stress fractures of bones can be likened to the cracks in a piece of wire which has been repeatedly bent – at first the wire looks strong but eventually, if stressed enough it can break right through.
(iii)   Group C.   Complete ruptures of muscles, tendons and ligaments, fractured or broken bones and dislocated joints.

Fig 59   Physiological representation of the knee.

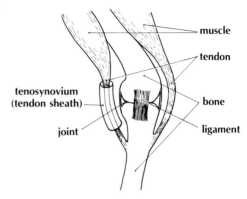

Further classification of injury can be as shown below:

Extrinsic (outside force)	*Intrinsic* (internal force)
collisions	incidental (no cause)
falls	overuse
equipment	acute
	chronic

AVOIDANCE OF INJURIES

The basic rule for avoiding injury is to increase your own fitness through increased speed, strength, endurance and flexibility, as outlined in Chapter 2. Using the training programme in a sensible, progressive way reduces the chances of sustaining intrinsic and overuse injuries. Skill is not only important in making a better all-round player but also enables the player to avoid injury through inappropriate technique. It is important to teach and practice good tackling techniques, blocking a ball and passing with either side of the foot and with both feet. Heading the ball requires special attention, especially when the ball is wet and perhaps heavy. Goalkeepers need to practise landing from dives when attempting to save the ball especially when playing on hard ground and artificial surfaces.

Warm-Up and Cool-Down

Warm-up is essential not only in preparation for matches but also in training. By gradually increasing the intensity of work and building up the number of skills to be rehearsed, the body and mind are both being warmed up (*see* Chapter 2). The muscles are controlled by electrical impulses fed to them from the brain and this system needs tuning and adjusting – just as the muscles need warming up. Equally important is the cool-down, when more emphasis is put on flexibility in order to test for any minor injury that may have occurred during exercise.

Gentle rhythmic movement also helps to flush out the waste products of metabolism from the muscles that have built up during high intensity exercise. Muscle stiffness the following day may be reduced by performing a regular post-match or post-training drill of stretching and low-intensity exercise (*see* Chapter 2).

Protection

Most extrinsic injuries can be avoided by taking sensible precautions and checking the safety of the training venue and any equipment that is to be used. Gyms should be well ventilated, well lit and with any sharp edges, radiators or walls padded with foam. Doors and windows should be secured and other recreational equipment stored correctly and well out of the way of the training area.

The pitch must be checked before each match or training session (and especially carefully at the beginning of the season) to make sure no sharp stones, glass or metal objects have been left on the grass. Touch flags must be easily knocked over when hit. Weight-training equipment should only be used under supervision and all users should be familiar with safety procedures.

The ball should be of the approved type; heavy balls may cause injuries to the feet, knees and head. Children may need to start with lighter, smaller, plastic balls. Clothing should be well fitting, not too tight (causing abrasions) nor too loose (restricting free movement) and tops should be long-sleeved to prevent friction burns.

When playing on artificial surfaces, shin-guards will reduce not only the number of sore legs but also broken legs by reducing impact. Boots should fit well; wear new boots for short periods in training only until they feel comfortable in order to cut down on blisters. Make sure you choose the right footwear for the right surface – you may need to have a different pair each for grass, artificial surfaces and wooden floors in gymnasiums. You should always remove dentures and on no account should you ever chew gum when either training or playing.

Some players may wish to strap their fingers, ankles or feet, particularly if they have been injured in the past. The strapping must not be elastic so that joints are adequately supported and must be removed after exercise allowing a full range of movement to take place. A trained physiotherapist can show you how to apply the tape.

Self-Control

The rules of the game and the regulations controlling the use of training venues have been devised not only to ensure fair play but also to prevent injury; it is therefore prudent to observe these rules for your own safety. It is especially important to play with and against people of your own physique and standard.

The tactics of play and set pieces from free kicks need to be learned and rehearsed with the coach and other players in order to reach a better understanding within the team. Self-control plays an important role in preventing and reducing injury. Try to organise your day so that there is adequate time for meals, allowing at least two hours to elapse after a large meal before training (see Chapter 3). Most athletes need a minimum of eight hours sleep each night and time must also be allocated for training, eating, studying or working. Fatigue will set in if not enough time is allowed for adequate rest between training sessions and this is one of the biggest causes of sports injuries as well as skill breakdown.

Regular showering or bathing after training and frequent washing of kit will help reduce the incidence of fungal infections of the skin. Do not borrow other people's clothing or towels and make sure you always have clean, dry clothing to change into after a training session. Athletes should be non-smokers, not only for obvious health reasons but also because the nicotine in cigarettes attaches itself to the oxygen-carrying component of the red blood cells (haemoglobin) thus reducing the available space for oxygen to be transported to the muscles. This effect lasts for up to three weeks after the last cigarette has been smoked.

By tradition many soccer players drink alcohol not only after but sometimes before a match. Alcohol should never be consumed before a match or training session – not only to avoid errors of judgement but also because alcohol dehydrates the body and makes it perform less efficiently. After a hard match or training session, particularly in hot conditions, plain fluid should be drunk first before racing to the bar.

Check-List for Injury Prevention

(i)   Environment: clothes; boots; equipment; surfaces; shin-guards.
(ii)   Control: training/match rules; physique; tactics.
(iii)   Fitness: skill; strength; speed; endurance; flexibility.
(iv)   Self-discipline: warm-up; diet; sleep; smoking; hygiene; alcohol.

MEDICAL PROBLEMS

Frequently it may be illness and not injury that prevents the sportsperson from training. Any soccer player who has an infection, such as a heavy cold, a chest infection or flu, should not train or play, especially if the body temperature is elevated above normal (36.9°C, 98.4°F) or if the resting pulse rate is appreciably higher than normal. You will not be able to perform well and certainly will not get any beneficial training effect if you continue to train at this stage; you also run the risk of the infection getting worse and the heart muscle being affected (myocarditis). Rest is essential until the illness passes. Low-grade chronic infections of the teeth, skin or sinuses, for example, may prevent you performing at peak level and treatment should be sought earlier rather than later. Some virus infections such as glandular fever may linger on for weeks and regrettably there is no treatment – so you must remain patient until the illness passes, returning gradually to full training.

Tetanus, or lockjaw, is an uncommon but severe illness which can be picked up from the soil through cuts and abrasions. Players should be vaccinated against tetanus and have a booster injection at least every ten years.

Dehydration

A reduction in body-weight of one per cent through lost sweat results in a ten per cent reduction in work capacity; likewise a two per cent loss will result in a twenty per cent reduction. It is therefore vital that any sweat lost is adequately and promptly replaced by water, not only to enhance performance, but also to prevent injury. Some people (particularly when training regularly in hot gyms or at the end of summer) may become chronically dehydrated with a subsequent reduction in body-weight, reduced urine output and a rise in resting pulse. Regular weighing and checking of the volume and colour of the urine should ensure that dehydration does not become a problem – thirst alone is not a reliable indicator of dehydration.

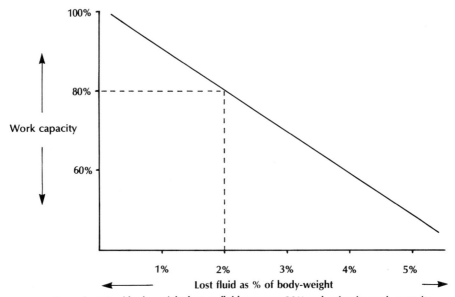

Example: 2% of body-weight lost as fluid causes a 20% reduction in work capacity

Fig 60   The relationship between the loss of body fluid and reduction in work capacity.

OVERTRAINING

This condition is difficult to spot and may creep up on the player and coach without either being aware of what is happening. It usually occurs when the player increases the training load both in frequency and intensity, not allowing time enough to eat, sleep, study or work. As the performance drops off the athlete tries to compensate by increasing the training load only to suffer further deterioration in performance, starting down the slippery slope and getting involved in a vicious circle of increased work and poor performance. The only cure is to rest for four days and increase both the fluid and carbohydrate intake, resisting the temptation to restart training after only one or two days when feeling a little recovered.

WOMEN

Women who have frequent heavy periods may lose enough iron to make themselves anaemic. When anaemia occurs the red blood cells are unable to carry sufficient oxygen to the muscles, resulting in tiredness both on and off the pitch. The doctor can easily correct this deficiency and advice should be sought as early as possible. Some women who undergo a lot of endurance training may cease to have any periods, particularly if they reduce their body fat. This condition is known as amenorrhoea and is quite normal in these circumstances; periods will return when the training load is decreased. Pregnant women can safely continue to train until they start feeling uncomfortable, indeed regular exercise in pregnancy results in healthier babies and easier childbirth for the mother. Playing competitive games is however, best avoided in order to decrease the risk of miscarriage due to body contact.

CHILDREN

Bones continue to grow up to the age of about eighteen in males and about sixteen in females. However, during growth the bones are not strong enough for the muscles and tendons attached to them, so heavy weight-training and repetitive high-load training should not be performed by pre-pubertal children. In some children the points at which tendons are attached to bones become inflamed, swollen and tender. This may happen just below the knee (Osgood–Schlatter's condition) or at the back of the heel (Sever's condition). Boys of twelve and fourteen years and girls between ten and twelve may develop Osgood–Schlatter's; if so they then complain of pain just below the knee when vigorously kicking the ball. They should be allowed to continue to play but should avoid long hard kicks and kicks from the penalty spot. The only treatment is to reduce the loading to that particular point, by cutting down on the training until the condition settles. The child can train on resilient surfaces such as grass and during training the use of shock-absorbing heel inserts made of sorbothane will prove effective in relieving pain. Children develop power and explosive force after puberty and so power-training should not be undertaken until after this time. Training with very light weights will, however, help with the technical skills of heavier weight-training later on.

VETERANS

Older sportspeople are not especially prone to particular injuries, but as age advances the chance of their being injured increases and the longer it takes them to recover from injury. If you go back to soccer later in life, having had a few years away from the sport, start gently with a gradual increase in the frequency and intensity of each session. Secondary injuries may occur in joints previously damaged in earlier years, for example, an injury such as osteoarthritis of the knee joint may develop long after a torn cartilage has been removed. These secondary injuries may prevent you from doing as much training as you would like, but you will have to adjust to this, perhaps supplementing your usual training with swimming and cycling.

TRAVEL

When travelling away from home, whether abroad or in your own country, you may experience difficulty in sleeping especially during the first few nights. A mild sleeping pill may prove helpful at this time and your doctor should be able to help if it becomes a problem. Stay clear of new and untried exotic foods, keep to your usual diet if at all possible and wash any fruit and salads in *clean* water before eating them. Check that the water supply is safe to drink and if not, consume bottled water only. When going to a hot climate the body takes ten days or so to acclimatise to the heat. After this period the salt content of the sweat is reduced and stabilised so all that is required is a little extra salt during the first few days (not salt tablets which can make you feel ill).

If you have a fair skin, you should keep out of the sun, and even if you tan easily you should still avoid sunbathing as you may become dehydrated. Ideally you should always wear long sleeves and long trousers at dusk and at dawn, to avoid insect bites and try to use plenty of insect repellent. Check with your doctor to find out whether any special vaccinations are required – well in advance of your trip. A travel check-list will include: vaccinations, food, water, heat acclimatisation, sleep disturbance and jet lag.

DOPING

It is your responsibility as a player to ensure that you do not abuse the drug-testing regulations, either intentionally or by error. Mistakes can occur when over-the-counter pain killers, cough mixtures, anti-diarrhoea medicines and nasal decongestants are used which may contain small amounts of codeine and ephedrine. Both drugs are on the banned list and will show up in urine as a positive dope test. Check with the governing body or the Sports Council's Drugs Advisory Group for an up-to-date list of drugs you can and cannot take.

FIRST AID

Resuscitation

If you are a coach you have a responsibility to know the basic procedures of resuscitation. When a serious casualty occurs your first aim is to save life before worrying about the extent of any sports injury:

(i)   Check the airway and remove any object which might be preventing air entering the lungs; remove any false teeth or mouth guards, clear the mouth of vomit or chewing gum and loosen any clothing around the throat. Extend the neck fully in order to prevent the tongue flopping down against the back of the throat.

(ii)   Check that the casualty is now breathing; if not, start CPR (cardio-pulmonary resuscitation) by giving the kiss of life. Breathe into the mouth of the casualty at the same time as pinching his or her nose to prevent air escaping from it.

(iii)   Check the circulation by feeling for a pulse; if you cannot detect it, start compressing the chest wall firmly four times for each of your breaths until the casualty starts breathing and regains his or her pulse, or until the ambulance arrives.

(iv)   After the patient has regained consciousness or started breathing by him or herself, check for any bleeding. If there is bleeding, apply firm pressure with a gauze swab or handkerchief for five minutes (in most cases this will be sufficient to stop blood loss from major vessels). You can then start assessing the extent of any injury and try to relieve pain by placing the casualty in a stable position on their side, splinting any obvious fractures. Ideally you should also have checked beforehand where the nearest telephone is; you must send someone to summon the ambulance in order to evacuate the injured person.

Treatment of Sports Injuries

The aim of treatment is to reduce the amount of damage already done, relieve pain and promote healing. When a sports injury or soft tissue injury occurs, small blood vessels become torn and blood escapes causing bruising and swelling. Actions should be taken to help reduce the amount of blood escaping and so cut down on the size of the swelling both of which hinder repair and rehabilitation. A mnemonic (RICE) is useful in this context:

Rest
Ice
Compression
Elevation

Rest is required for the first twenty-four hours following an injury in order to prevent further bleeding.

Ice is applied to the injury for ten minutes every two hours in the first twenty-four hours. This reduces pain, swelling and further bleeding. The ice should be wrapped in a damp tea-towel and must not come into direct contact with the skin; if it does an ice burn may occur. If ice is not available, cold water from the tap will suffice as will a bag of frozen peas from the freezer!

Compression of the injury by a firmly applied crepe bandage prevents further blood loss and reduces the size of any swelling. The bandage should not be too tight and you may need to re-apply the crepe in the first twenty-four hours if it becomes too loose or too tight.

Elevation assists in the 'drainage' of swelling and prevents further blood loss. The affected limb is raised above heart level for twenty-four hours.

Treatment of Blisters

The treatment for blisters depends upon whether or not the skin overlying it is intact. If it is, the blister should be left alone, but if the skin has been broken the blister should be 'deroofed' with a clean pair of scissors. This prevents infection setting in and also assists in the blister bed healing more rapidly, if perhaps a little more uncomfortably in the short term. While training, the blister should be covered with a dry, non-absorbent dressing, held in place by a piece of tape or strapping. While on the subject of first aid, the contents of any first-aid box should contain: crepe bandages, gauze squares, zinc oxide tape, plasters, cotton wool, triangular bandage, scissors, antiseptic solution, analgesic (pain killing) tablets, collar, splints. You should also have access to a stretcher, blanket and Brooks airway.

REHABILITATION

Early rehabilitation of most injuries should be encouraged in order to shorten the time taken to reach a full recovery. In the first twenty-four hours when 'RICE' is applied, gentle passive movements are made, to assist in the drainage of any swelling and to prevent blood clots forming in the deep veins. After a further twenty-four hours, more active stretching exercises are performed followed by strengthening exercises. The muscles around an injury rapidly lose power and the co-ordination of muscle movements also worsens within a few hours of the injury being sustained. As the muscles regain power, re-education of soccer skills becomes a priority eventually allowing a return to training and to playing matches.

Models for Rehabilitation

(i)   Group A injuries.
Bruising only has occurred and all that is generally required is the application of RICE in the first twenty-four hours followed by a fairly rapid resumption of normal training.

(ii)   Group B injuries.
(a)   Ligaments/joints. A sprained ligament on the outside of the ankle joint is one of the more common soccer injuries. The principles used for the rehabilitation of this particular injury may also be applied to similar injuries to other parts of the body.

After the first twenty-four hours (when RICE is applied) you should try to walk on the injured side without a limp in order to stretch any scar tissue that is forming into its correct anatomical alignment. Initially this may mean that you will have to walk very slowly, before progressing first to normal walking pace and then to walking and jogging on grass five to ten metres at a time, slowly increasing the distance to twenty-five, fifty, seventy-five and then one hundred metres. When you have reached this stage, continue jogging for up to four hundred metres before starting a few sprints of five to ten metres followed by sprints of twenty-five, fifty, seventy-five and one hundred metres. Now run backwards and start weaving and jumping to strengthen the ankle further. Now start dribbling a ball and then begin to kick the ball further and further, working towards a full kick.

Nerves are damaged in a ligament injury and so lose their ability to tell the brain where in space the foot is. These nerves need to be re-educated and the best way to do so is by doing balance exercises. These positional or 'proprioceptive' exercises must be done at the same time as the stretching and strengthening drills. Start by trying to 'stork-stand' on your injured leg and then close your eyes. After this try throwing a tennis ball up into the air and catching it again while still balancing on one leg. The degree of difficulty can be increased by standing on a balance or wobble board. When you can do all of this quite happily for fifteen to twenty minutes you are then fit enough to resume normal training with your squad or team. However, if having done this your ankle still does not feel stable or if you are unable to play, you should seek advice from a sports clinic or qualified physiotherapist.

(b)   Muscles and tendons. Torn thigh muscles (quadriceps) may occur in soccer when kicking vigorously or landing awkwardly from a jump. The aim of rehabilitation is to prevent shortening of the muscle or tendon by inappropriate scar tissue formation (scar tissue may contract for several weeks after an injury).

Following the usual RICE application in the first twenty-four hours you should gently stretch the quadriceps muscle each morning and evening and for a minute every hour during the day. As gentle stretching becomes less uncomfortable, more active stretching and static strengthening exercises should be undertaken followed by dynamic exercises with increased loadings. Accordingly, start with straight-leg exercises, then bend the knee and then add weights of one to two kilograms, attached to the ankle while bending and straightening the knee.

After this the routine of jogging, sprinting, weaving, running backwards and dribbling a ball, together with balance exercises (as used for the ankle injury) should be followed.

(iii)   **Group C injuries.**

Bone fractures and dislocated joints. Most fractures or broken bones, together with joint dislocations, are major injuries and will need a minimum of six weeks immobilisation before any rehabilitation can commence. They also require close medical supervision. Stress fractures, however, need only to be rested for three weeks before gentle progressive training is resumed. If you think you have a stress fracture you should stop training and seek medical advice.

Concussion

If a player is concussed (in other words the player has lost consciousness – however briefly – with or without memory loss) it is important to stop immediately and for the player to be examined by a doctor or sent to the nearest casualty department. The player should not be allowed to play again for *three weeks*. If the same person is unfortunate enough to be concussed again the period should be extended to six weeks and if for a third time in the same season, the player should not play again for four months.

5   Mental Training

It is ironic that despite the widespread recognition of mental factors in sport, very few practical training books on specific sports make more than a passing reference to mental training. Nevertheless, there are now quite a few books on mental training in sport, some of which are listed in Further Reading at the end of this book. The complete player, therefore, will be someone who trains physically *and* mentally.

In his book, *The Pursuit of Sporting Excellence* (1986), David Hemery recalls his numerous interviews with a wide range of sport's highest achievers. In response to his question 'to what extent was the mind involved in playing your sport?' he reported that 'the unanimous verdict was couched in words like "immensely", "totally", "that's the whole game", "you play with your mind", "that's where the body movement comes from" '. In short, we all recognise the importance of having the right mental approach in sport just as we recognise the importance of physical factors. The purpose of this chapter, therefore, is to present a selection of some mental training skills relevant to soccer players (in fact many of the skills are relevant to most people in a wide variety of sports). Before outlining some of these skills, it is important to dispel some of the myths surrounding mental training in sport.

MYTHS AND TRUTHS

Myth 1   'You only need a sports psychologist if you have mental problems.' If that was the case then, extending the argument, we would only need to train physically when we were trying to recover from injury! There is no difference between practising physical and mental skills – they should both be practised regularly as a positive aid to performance and not just to offset 'problems' (although they can usefully be employed for this as well).

Myth 2   'All good athletes have a natural mental toughness and don't need to practise mental skills.' Certainly some people will have better mental qualities than others (in exactly the same way that some people are more physically gifted than others). However, that does not mean that mental training will not help. Even people like Bryan Robson and Diego Maradonna have put in tremendous amounts of physical training even though they are clearly physically gifted people. These days natural ability is not enough.

Myth 3   'Mental skills cannot be trained or developed.' This is similar to the last myth and it too is incorrect. All skills, whether physical or mental can be improved with appropriate practice.

Mental training may not be fully accepted by all people in sport. However, the preceding argument may have convinced you that it is illogical to expect physical training to be the only type of football training when we all recognise that many games are won and lost on mental attitudes and abilities. Many years ago it was considered slightly odd – even 'unsporting' – to train more than about three days a week. That attitude has long since gone but has been replaced with a reluctance to accept regular mental training as a part of contemporary sport. In a few years time, perhaps, we will look back at such an odd attitude with a sense of amusement?

COMPONENTS OF MENTAL TRAINING

In Chapter 2 the various components of physical fitness training were outlined and it was stated then that fitness was best defined in terms of its constituent parts. In the same way, it would be naive to say that mental training is made up of just one factor. It is a term given to a number of different components, but it will not be possible to cover all of these in such a short space and interested readers should refer to Further Reading. What will be done here, however, is to outline the basic features of five topics which are:

(i)   relaxation and the control of stress;
(ii)   mental imagery;
(iii)   concentration and mental control;
(iv)   self-confidence;
(v)   team work.

The background to each of these areas will be explained in brief, including examples from football, and then some practical mental training exercises in each area will be outlined. However, it should be noted that not all mental skills can be taught easily by coaches without training, although the exercises outlined here have been chosen for simplicity and safety. It is recommended, however, that if mental skills are introduced, they should be done so first by a registered sports psychologist of the British Association of Sports Sciences (*see* Useful Addresses). Coaches are also advised to attend courses on sports psychology run by the National Coaching Foundation (whose address is also at the end of the book).

Relaxation and the Control of Stress

Relaxation is a much misunderstood concept in mental training – many players think that if relaxation skills are needed at all, they are needed just before a game. Clearly, being too relaxed is not a good idea, nor is being too tense. The answer, therefore, is to control the 'on–off switch' of the body. On most radios the on–off switch also controls the volume. As we are 'on' all of the time, the essence of controlling the on–off switch is to control the volume.

One way to do this is to learn relaxation skills, of which there are many. Other mental skills, such as mental imagery and concentration, are also dependent upon being able to control the relaxation and activation (arousal) of the body.

Relaxation not only facilitates rest and recovery in sport, but can also have a more immediate effect on performance through reducing anxiety and muscle tension. Moreover, this can relate to self-confidence – another mental skill to be discussed later.

Arousal is the 'intensity aspect' of our behaviour since we often refer to being under-aroused (e.g. drowsy, sleepy) or over-aroused (e.g. over-excited, panicky). In sport it is easy to get over-aroused with the excitement of the situation. This can often be captured in amusing illustrations such as the Rugby player who is so 'psyched-up' at the kick-off that he charges down the field only to discover that he has over-run the ball by 30 metres! This shows that over-arousal is not necessarily a good thing in sport and can badly affect concentration.

There are many different types of relaxation skill that can be learned, including breathing exercises, muscle tense–relax exercises and meditation. After a time you will develop your own preference if exposed to the different types and there is no one technique that can be recommended more than another. Two techniques will be outlined here, and others can be found in the books listed in the Further Reading section. It should be recognised that not everyone is suited to starting these exercises, especially those with abnormal blood pressure, a history of cardiorespiratory health problems, asthmatics and those suffering acute anxiety states, who should all be referred to their doctor beforehand.

Deep Muscle Relaxation

This simple technique requires you to lie on a mat on the floor with your arms and legs stretched out. Gradually reduce your breathing rate to a slow yet comfortable rate, start saying the word 'relax' to yourself as you breathe out. Close your eyes when you feel ready to do so, but do not force it. After about ten exhalations coupled with the word 'relax', focus your attention on your left leg. Imagine it getting gradually heavier and heavier as you become increasingly relaxed. Imagine your leg sinking into the mat (concentrate on this for about a minute). Now shift your attention to your right leg and repeat the exercise. This can also be done for your left and right arms in succession. After this you should be quite relaxed and feeling 'heavy' – with little or no muscular tension. Slowly sit up, stretch and return to normal activities.

This should be practised for short spells initially as your concentration is likely to be poor. Five minutes may not sound very much but will be long enough for the first session. This form of deep relaxation is best performed several hours before a match to allow you plenty of time to increase the arousal level to the appropriate point for the match.

Progressive Muscle Relaxation

Progressive muscle relaxation (PMR) is a well-known technique for learning the difference between relaxation and tension. It was developed in the 1930s by Edmund Jacobsen and is widely used in sport, health and other contexts today. Essentially, the technique is built upon the premise that you will be unable to relax effectively until you can first recognise tension. Consequently, a series of tense-relax exercises are outlined which are designed to increase the awareness of muscular tension and relaxation, as illustrated in Fig 61. Below there is a PMR script which you can either have read to you or which can be recorded in a quiet, relaxed voice.

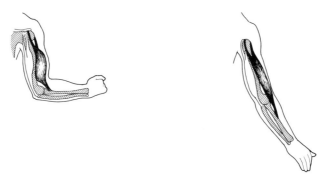

Fig 61 The tense–relax sequence of progressive muscle relaxation.

Relaxation Procedures

These procedures should be practised twice a day for about ten minutes at a time (evenings are often a good time to practise). The order of the steps involved is very important; however, the particular words or thoughts that the athlete uses to accomplish each step are not. For example, it is important that you relax prior to concentrating on bowling. When you are concentrating on relaxing your arms, we don't care if you say to yourself, 'Now I am going to release all the muscular tension in my hands, fingers, and forearms,' or if you say, 'Now I am going to relax the muscles in my hands, fingers, and arms.'

Prior to beginning the exercise, find a quiet, comfortable place where you will not be disturbed and where you can either sit or lie down. If you wear contact lenses, you may want to remove them. If you have on restrictive clothing (like a tie), you may want to loosen it. Make yourself comfortable with your hands at your sides or in your lap and you are ready to begin.

1   Close your eyes and take three deep breaths, inhaling and exhaling deeply and slowly. As you exhale, relax your entire body as much as you can. Continue to notice your breathing throughout the session. You will find that as you exhale, your relaxation will become deeper.

2   Now clench both of your fists. Close them and squeeze them tighter and tighter together. As you squeeze them, notice the tension in your forearms, your hands, and your fingers. That's fine, now let them go, relax them. Let your fingers become loose and notice the pleasant feeling of heaviness in your arms and hands as the tension disappears. Feel the heaviness of your arms and hands as they rest against your body or the chair. That's fine, try it one more time, clench both fists and feel the tension, squeeze harder, hold the tension, now let go and completely relax.

3   Now bend your elbows, clench your fists, and flex your biceps. Flex them harder, hold the tension and study it. Now unbend your elbows, relax your hands, get your arms back in a comfortable position, study how your arms feel as you completely let go and relax them.

4   Now straighten your arms and flex the triceps muscle in the back of your upper arms. Hold the tension, increase it, squeeze harder, study the tension. That's fine, now relax, return your arms to a comfortable position and enjoy the release from the tension. Enjoy the feelings, and even when you feel completely relaxed, try and let go even more.

5   Now clench your teeth, feel the muscles tightening in your neck and jaws. Once again, study the tension, clench your teeth tighter, tighter. Now relax your jaws, let your mouth open slightly, and feel your muscles loosen, feel the relief from the tension.

6   Pay attention to your neck muscles. Press your head back as far as it will go and feel the tension, now roll it straight to the right. Again feel the increase in the tension in your muscles. Move your head to the left, pressing hard and feeling the tension in your muscles. Hold the same position and study the tension. Now let your head move into a comfortable position and relax the muscles in your neck and shoulders. Notice the pleasant change as you feel the tension leaving your muscles. Pay attention to how your neck and shoulders feel when the muscles are relaxed.

7   Now pay attention to your breathing and relax your entire body. Breathe deeply and slowly, and as you exhale, relax all the muscles in your arms. Just let yourself go and completely relax. Let your mouth open slightly and relax the muscles in your face, jaw, and forehead. Relax the muscles in your neck and shoulders. . . Relax the muscles in your feet, your calves, and your thighs . . . That's fine . . . Just completely relax and let yourself go. Continue to breathe deeply and slowly, and enjoy the pleasant feeling of being completely relaxed.

8   At this time those of you who wish may practise rehearsing the sights and feelings that you associate with a particular pleasant activity. This practice should not last for more than four to five minutes.

9   Now, since you have relaxed so completely, it is best to take your time in moving around. Get out of this relaxed state by using three steps. First, count one and take a deep breath and hold it. Second, count two and stretch your arms and legs, then exhale. Third, count three and open your eyes. You should be wide awake and feeling very relaxed and comfortable.

Procedure Summary
1   Close your eyes and breathe deeply and slowly.
2   Relax the muscles in your forearms.
3   Relax your biceps.
4   Relax your triceps.
5   Relax your face, jaw, and forehead.
6   Relax your neck and shoulders.
7   Breathe slowly and relax your entire body.
8   Rehearse an activity.
9   Take a deep breath, stretch, and open your eyes.

Reprinted with permission from Nideffer, R.M., *The Inner Athlete* (Thomas Y. Crowell, 1976).

It is also possible to purchase relaxation tapes (available from the National Coaching Foundation). Fig 62 shows some of the exercises for PMR.

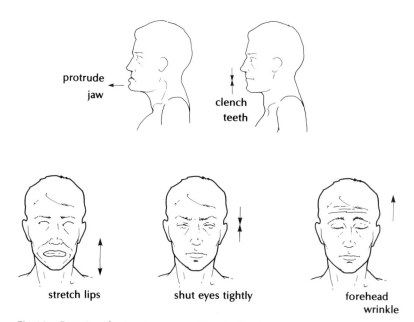

Fig 62   Exercises for tension recognition in PMR.

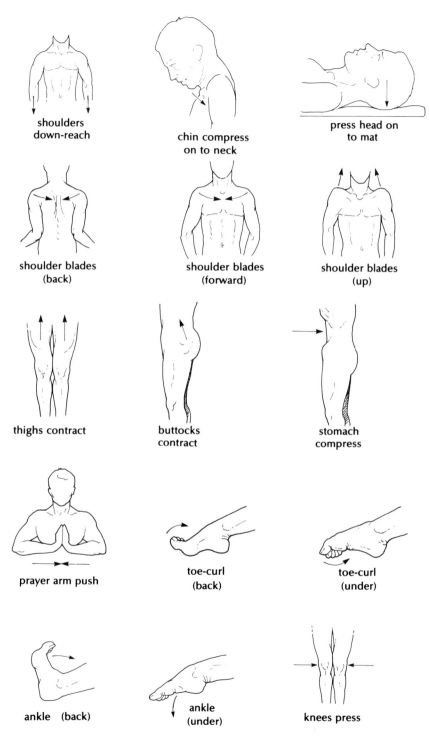

shoulders
down-reach

chin compress
on to neck

press head on
to mat

shoulder blades
(back)

shoulder blades
(forward)

shoulder blades
(up)

thighs contract

buttocks
contract

stomach
compress

prayer arm push

toe-curl
(back)

toe-curl
(under)

ankle (back)

ankle
(under)

knees press

Fig 62   Continued.

Relaxation, Anxiety and Stress

We have all experienced the unpleasantness of anxiety in sport; the nervousness before a big game, or the critical point in the match which could swing it either way. However, not all stress is bad. Stress actually refers to any situation when we are 'out of balance', such as when the task appears to be too difficult or too easy for us. (The latter will produce the stress of boredom, hence the diagram in Fig 63 which shows that optimum enjoyment is often the result of matching the challenge with the right level of skills; any imbalance could cause stress.) The body prepares for stress through the 'fight–flight' reaction, which is the response of the body preparing for action with increased heart rate, breathing rate, adrenalin flow and so on. This feeling could equally be fear or excitement depending upon how you see the situation. If you hear footsteps rapidly approaching you from behind in a dark alleyway late at night you will react with fear if you think it is a mugger. However, if you think it is a jogger you will not react in the same way. In other words, your stress or anxiety response depends on the way in which you see the situation. In soccer you will need to develop relaxation skills and a positive way of looking at the game whenever you become anxious.

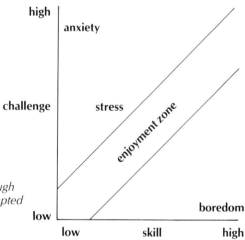

Fig 63   Optimal enjoyment through matching challenge and skill, adapted from Csikszentmihalyi, M., Beyond Boredom and Anxiety (Jossey-Bass, 1975).

Mental Imagery

The ability to visualise events and skills in football is another important mental skill which needs practice. It has been known for some time from psychology experiments that practising a skill mentally is better than not practising at all, although obviously the best situation is to combine physical with mental practice. But what is mental imagery?

Mental imagery is the repetition of a physical skill or movement sequence that is practised through thought and through pictures, rather than through actual physical movement. Although the exact reasons why mental imagery works are still not clearly understood, we do know that it does work. Experiments as long ago as the 1930s demonstrated that small electrical impulses could be detected in the muscles from thought alone. This suggests that the 'grooving in' of technique in sport can be accomplished, at least in part, by mental imagery. Obviously, such repetitive practice can only take place for predictable skills, such as some set piece moves. Equally, these set moves can be mentally rehearsed to aid memory as well as skill. It is more difficult, of course, to rehearse mentally the spontaneous movements that occur in an open team game such as football. However, by visualising such open play, and the options and decisions you may take in such situations, your confidence may well be developed.

Brent Rushall, a sports psychologist, lists six important guidelines for successful mental rehearsal in his book, *Psyching in Sport*:

(i)   your picture should be in the real environment. In other words, if you want to practise a penalty kick mentally then imagine yourself in a competitive situation – it is more realistic;
(ii)   perform the skill in full;
(iii)   make sure the visualisation is successful – avoid rehearsing errors (although this is easier said than done). With practice, though, you should improve the clarity of your mental image and find it easier to control;
(iv)   visualise the skill before actual performance;
(v)   imagine the skill at the normal speed;
(vi)   imagine the skill visually and kinesthetically. In other words, try to feel the movement as if actually performing it. This is best done by visualising yourself actually performing rather than apparently watching yourself on a video. More useful advice can be found in John Syer and Christopher Connolly's book *Sporting Body, Sporting Mind.* They suggest that visualisation should follow these guidelines:

(i)   start with relaxation;
(ii)   stay alert;
(iii)   use the present tense;
(iv)   set realistic and specific goals (*see* later in this chapter);
(v)   use all of your senses;
(vi)   visualise at the correct speed;
(vii)   practise regularly;
(viii) enjoy it!

Answer the questionnaire in Fig 64 after your initial attempts at mental imagery. This should highlight some of your problem areas for you to work on next time. Remember, keep the initial sessions short and relax beforehand.

TICK ONE

	Yes	In Between	No
(i) Could you 'see' and 'feel' yourself perform the skill?			
(ii) Could you control the picture?			
(iii) Was the picture clear?			
(iv) Was the skill executed successfully?			
(v) Was the skill at normal speed?			
(vi) Did you stay relaxed?			
(vii) Did you stay alert?			
(viii) Did you use senses other than just 'sight' and 'feel'?			

Fig 64 Mental imagery questionnaire. Answer the questions after each of your initial training sessions with mental imagery.

Concentration and Mental Control

We all recognise the importance of concentration but rarely actually practise it as a skill. Try this exercise now, but before doing so ensure that you have space around you – for example make sure that there is no furniture that you could hit if you fall over. It is also a good idea to have someone with you just in case you do start to fall over.

(i)   Stand upright with your hands on your hips, eyes looking forward. Now take one foot off the ground and rest it against the other shin. How long can you keep your balance without moving the foot that is in contact with the ground?
(ii)   Try the same exercise again, this time with your eyes closed. How long can you keep your balance this time?
(iii)   Finally, try it again, but this time close your eyes and tip your head back. How long can you keep your balance now?

It is probable that your balance deteriorated as you tried these exercises in turn. But why? These exercises each required concentration to maintain balance, but they became more difficult because they gave you less to concentrate on each time. The first exercise allowed you to have your eyes open, so balance was maintained by concentrating on a combination of seeing and feeling – this is not very difficult because it is the way we operate in normal life. In the second exercise you were deprived of sight and so only had feeling to help you. If you did not concentrate totally on the small deviations of balance, you probably fell. Finally, in the third variation, the balance mechanisms (in the inner ear) were disturbed by tilting your head back and so, unless you could concentrate superbly on the limited feedback you were getting, you easily lost your balance.

What these exercises illustrate is that in sport, concentration means the ability to focus on the details around you that are needed for the game and to exclude those which are extraneous. In soccer you need to focus on the ball rather than the reaction of people watching on the sidelines. Many of the top sportspeople interviewed in David Hemery's book *The Pursuit of Sporting Excellence* rated concentration as a very important factor for them.

A simple exercise to develop concentration is to sit, comfortable and relaxed in a chair, and to close your eyes. Then start counting with each exhalation starting at one and counting with each breath. You need to maintain a state of 'relaxed concentration' to get to the high numbers. Alternately, why not try the balance exercises again? Now that you know what to concentrate on you should be more successful.

Focusing Your Attention

Part of sports concentration, as has already been suggested, is the ability to attend to the right things at the right time. Fig 65 illustrates the process of attention in sport and shows that attention is made up of at least two parts – direction and focus. The direction of attention is the internal–external line on the diagram and refers to the extent we attend to things internally (such as thoughts and feelings) or externally (objects in our environment). The other line in Fig 65 is the focus or width of attention (broad–narrow) and refers to whether our attention is narrowly focused (on the ball) or broadly focused (on the changing defensive pattern of the opposition). Four main types of attention can therefore be extracted from Fig 65 and applied to different situations in soccer.

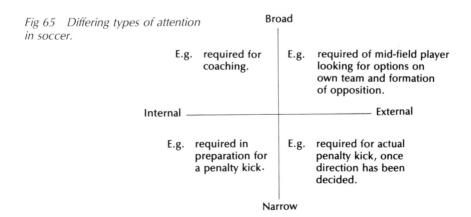

Fig 65   Differing types of attention in soccer.

The top left square is the broad–internal (analysis) style of attention required by the coach, who needs to be able to see things in a broad way – such as the way the entire team is functioning – but at the same time focus internally on thoughts and feelings about the way the game is going, possible changes to be made at half-time and so on. The top right square is the broad–external (assessment) focus of attention required by all footballers. For example, they not only have to adjust to the way the ball is passed to them (requiring an external focus), but must also be aware of the opposition tacklers and the positions of fellow players (broad focus).

The lower right square refers to the external–narrow (action) focus needed during the execution of a specific skill, such as a long kick. This is because kickers, once committed, should focus on their own body movement and skill (narrow) as well as where the ball is to be placed. Finally, the lower left square is internal–narrow and is the focus of attention needed for the preparation of a skill. In soccer this might occur just prior to taking a penalty kick when attention should be focused narrowly on the exact skill itself.

An American psychologist, Robert Nideffer, who devised the model in Fig 65, suggests that it is not important just to adopt the right focus of attention at the right time, but that it is also critical to be able to *shift* attention from one square to the next as appropriate. Many people in sport are unable to do this effectively because they have a 'preferred style' and tend to stick to it. Clearly, this leads to errors in the game and players and coaches should work on attentional focus and this ability to shift attention. For example, after a score the player could shift to an internal–narrow focus in order to control tension, and then quickly shift to a broad–external style to see where other players are positioned. Further detail can be found in Nideffer's mental training manual listed in the Further Reading section.

Self-Confidence

Self-confidence is one of the key areas of mental training for sport. It is very rare indeed for successful sports people to have a persistent lack of self-confidence. In understanding self-confidence, four main factors need to be identified. These are: prior performance; demonstration and imitation; verbal persuasion and positive self-talk; and monitoring arousal. The most powerful source of confidence is likely to be your past performance and since success will lead to confidence and vice versa, a 'positive confidence cycle' can be set up. If your sports performance is improving then all is fine, but what can you do when your performance is declining? How can you break into the confidence cycle? One technique which has been shown to be effective is goal-setting (which will be considered later in this chapter).

The second source of confidence is observation and imitation of others. Coaches can organise highly effective learning situations for soccer players through the use of demonstrations, films and so forth which can act as confidence-building sessions. For example, a player lacking confidence in tackling can benefit from watching someone perform the skill successfully.

(However, it is not always such a good idea to show constantly the 'ideal' skill executed by the best player as this may deflate confidence with players saying to themselves 'I'll never be able to do it like that!') Live and recorded demonstrations have been found to be effective, as well as techniques which physically assist players to adopt the correct positions. This is more usual in sports such as gymnastics but could be used for some of the skills in soccer. In addition, players may build confidence through imagining correct skills, so highlighting again the importance of mental imagery.

A third source of confidence is verbal persuasion from others, although this may be a relatively weak source of confidence, depending upon the people involved; certainly encouragement from a highly respected person can help. A better source of persuasion is likely to come from within the player. Confidence-building statements are sometimes referred to as 'positive self-talk' or 'affirmations'. The most famous one in sport is Mohammed Ali's 'I am the greatest!' Although it may sound odd, there are plenty of examples of people gaining confidence from saying positive things to themselves. Three techniques for developing positive self-talk and affirmations are given in Fig 66.

A further source of self-confidence can be found in the physiological arousal of the body. If the 'stress response' (referred to earlier) is thought to indicate negative feelings such as fear, then arousal will reduce confidence. A typical reaction here would be for the player, at a critical time in the game, to say 'I can feel my heart pounding. Hell, I'm scared!' Conversely, if the person sees their reaction differently, it could become a positive influence. For example, the player could say, 'I can feel my heart pounding. That's great! I'm ready for this!' Changing such negative thoughts into positive ones can be a useful confidence strategy.

Technique	Method	Comments
'As if' visualisation	Imagine you are someone or something which creates confidence for you. Example: imagine that you are ten feet tall when heading.	You can add a positive slogan (see below) to go with this exercise.
Positive slogans	Think of a slogan which, when you see it, gives you confidence and direction.	Write it on a card and keep it in a prominent place.
Special words	Think of key or special words which are likely to help confidence, such as 'STROKE' as you control a pass to a team mate.	

Fig 66 Techniques for developing confidence through words and images (based on Syer and Connolly's Sporting Body, Sporting Mind).

Goal-Setting

One of the best ways to develop confidence and build sound psychological principles into your training is to use goal-setting. Although many people in sport use some kind of planning which approximates to the setting of goals, probably little thought has gone into the best ways of utilising goal-setting. Before outlining a simple goal-setting exercise for football players, the following guidelines should be noted:

(i)   Goals can be set for the short-term, medium-term or long-term. To help immediate motivation and action, short-term goals are best.

(ii)   Goals should be specific and measureable. Just to set the goal of 'improving my tackling' does not give enough direction. Set a goal that is highly specific and can be measured for success. Feedback based on such measurements is crucial for successful goal-setting.

(iii)   Goals should be realistic but challenging. It is easy to set very high goals, but disappointment will set in if they are not reached. On the other hand, very easy goals will not create extra motivation and direction.

(iv)   Goals should be accepted and worth while. For goals to be effective they must be accepted by the participant (hence it is best for the player to be involved in the goal-setting process rather than simply the coach), and considered worth the effort involved.

Fig 67 shows a goal-setting example for a soccer player. Study this and then complete your own using the structure in Fig 68.

Long term goal	Goals for next month	Goals and action for this week
To be the number one striker in the club.	To perform eight out of ten successful one against one drills and against a real opponent.	(i) To spend ten mins each session practising one against one drills with emphasis on beating your opponent. (ii) To hit designated 'spaces' in the goal with at least eight out of ten shots.

Fig 67   Examples of goal-setting in soccer.

Long term goal	Goals for next month	Goals and action for this week
		(i) (ii)
		(i) (ii)
		(i) (ii)

Fig 68   Your goal-setting chart.

Team-Work

The final topic for mental training that will be considered here refers to team-work. There is no magic formula for getting teams to work well together, although some guidelines may help. Further details can be found in *Sporting Body, Sporting Mind* by Syer and Connolly.

Understanding Others

A key to effective team-work is understanding why other people are playing the game – it may come as a surprise that people do not play football for the same reasons. Three main reasons have been identified in the past:

(i)   To play to win.
(ii)   To play well and demonstrate skill.
(iii)   To be part of a team.

Clearly these reasons will exist in players in varying degrees and some may be interested in all three. Nevertheless, coaches, team leaders and others may find that knowing their colleagues' main reasons for playing could help relationships within the team and between players and coaches. For example, the player wanting to demonstrate skills will be far less tolerant of sitting on the bench during the game than the person who is happy just being a team member.

Team Togetherness

It is often assumed that teams that are cohesive will play better. Although there have been exceptions, this is generally true. However, the cohesion of the team is not a simple matter – players have different personalities and will react differently in various situations. The group 'psych-up', therefore, is likely only to work for some of the players.

It is best to view group cohesion in two ways. Firstly, the extent to which players view the team as a whole (cohesion, togetherness, unity and so forth) and secondly, the degree of attraction the individual player has to the group. Both of these can have two 'orientations', or ways of working – task and social. A task orientation is where the focus is on getting the job done. This would mean that the team is primarily motivated to play well and win, rather than to enjoy each other's company. A social orientation, on the other hand, is geared towards social relationships rather than group performance. One would expect a social orientation to be stronger in more 'casual' teams and a task orientation to be stronger in high-level or professional teams, although there is no reason why most teams should not possess an interest in both orientations to some degree.

Team Meetings

John Syer and Christopher Connolly have identified three types of team meetings that may be useful in developing mental skills for teams:

(i)   Pre-game meetings. These are for the team to warm up in the emotional and psychological sense. They should be short and to the point. However, not all players will want a highly excitable 'psych-up'.
(ii)   Post-game discussion meetings. These are held at the training session after a competitive game to discuss the team's performance and to plan for the future. Group goal-setting can take place here.
(iii)   Team spirit meetings. Numerous discussion topics may be aired, although this meeting will probably not take place very often.

One aspect of mental training that should help the team effort is that if every player in the team makes a commitment to mental training, then this in itself should assist the cohesiveness and 'togetherness' of the team.

POSTSCRIPT

Thus we see that mental training provides a positive step forward towards becoming a more complete soccer player. Everyone will be doing it in the years to come, so why not get a 'head' start?

6 Summary and Programme Planning

In this book we have attempted to provide coverage of the major areas of training for soccer. These are:

(i)   Skill development.
(ii)   Physical fitness.
(iii)   Nutrition.
(iv)   Injury prevention.
(v)   Mental training.

Of course it is not easy to fit all of these into a day-to-day training programme. However, each of these should form part of the regular ongoing training programme and two in particular – injury prevention and nutrition – should underpin each session. So, having acquired this wisdom, you now need some guidelines for implementing the programme.

ASSESSMENT

A useful start is to assess your current level of training and performance. Only then can a proper 'prescription' and planning exercise take place. For example, assessment may show that you are relatively poor in speed and in the skill of heading. These would then feature more extensively in your training programme. On a more general level, the training plan should follow the structure below:

(i)   End of season recovery.
(ii)   Preparation phase I (out of season).
(iii)   Preparation phase II (pre-season).
(iv)   Competition phase.

The emphasis in each phase is shown in Fig 69. This outlines no more than a basic plan and it is likely that different players will have to adapt this to meet their own needs. However, in terms of 'peaking', league matches prevent this being a desirable or attainable strategy. In leagues, early season form needs to be high and then maintained. However, for cup competition it is possible to build up to a peak nearer the latter stages of the event. If this is the case then the emphasis should shift back to period 3 (preparation phase II) for the early rounds to peaking in period 4 (the competition phase). Do not try to stay with

Training component	PERIOD			
	1	2	3	4
Mental training	[rest or diversion from soccer]	**	***	***
Aerobic training		***	***	**
Strength		**	**	*
Muscular endurance		***	**	**
Power		*	***	***
Speed		*	***	***
Flexibility		**	**	**
Individual skills		***	***	***
Team skills		*	**	***

Period 1 End of season recovery (up to 2 weeks).
Period 2 Preparatory phase I, out of season (about 2 months).
Period 3 Preparatory phase II, pre-season (about 1 month).
Period 4 Competition phase (about 8 months).

*** very important
 ** important
  * lower priority (maintenance)

Fig 69   Planning your training throughout the year.

the training schedules of period 4 for too long as staleness or 'burn-out' may occur.

These days soccer is such a popular game that the summer break seems to get shorter each year. For this reason it is difficult to fit in all out-of-season and pre-season training. The key point to remember here is that not all matches can be treated as cup finals and hard training may have to take place prior to matches in order to reap the benefits for more important matches later on. It is usual to change the pattern of training throughout the year to get the best results when they are most needed. This is called 'periodisation' or 'cycling' the training year by doing different exercises at different times. The main reasons for using periodisation are:

(i)   To vary the training load.
(ii)   To aid recovery.
(iii)   To achieve peak performance at a desired time.

This is particularly important for more advanced players who need to peak for specific matches, although beginners, too, should have variety in training.

Level	Physical fitness	Skill training	Mental training
Beginner	Foundation principles across all components.	Basic individual techniques; later team skills for the club player.	Relaxation, arousal control and goal-setting.
Intermediate	Basic components plus emphasis on weaknesses and special needs.	Development of advanced skills.	Problem-solving skills and group skills.
Advanced	Specialised intensive training.	Maintenance and development of individual skills; advanced group skills.	Self-sufficiency in mental skills; advanced individual techniques and group skills.

Fig 70   Training patterns for soccer players of different levels.

A BALANCED PROGRAMME

A balanced training programme is important for all soccer players. The game itself requires skill, fitness, mental skills, and many more qualities.

CONCLUSION

There is no such player as the 'complete footballer'! However, it is to be hoped that you can get closer to fulfilling your own goals of personal improvement and enjoyment through a higher standard of football by implementing the training ideas from this book.

Glossary

Aerobic   'With oxygen'; used to describe 'steady-state' exercise where the body relies on oxygen as a continuous source of fuel.

Amenorrhoea   Absence of normal female monthly cycle or periods.

Amino Acid   The constituent parts of protein: eight of these acids cannot be made in the body (these are termed essential) and must form part of our diet. Another twelve can be synthesised in the body.

Anaemia   A deficiency of red blood cells, or of their haemoglobin. Most likely to occur in women with heavy periods or otherwise due to insufficient iron replacement.

Anaerobic   'Without oxygen'; used to describe the energy systems of the body which are used in short, high-intensity exercise.

Basal Metabolic Rate   A term used to describe the absolute amount of energy required to maintain the body function for life. It is a very precise measure made when the subject is awake, at perfect rest, 12 hours after a meal and in a thermoneutral environment.

Bending the Ball   To swerve the ball around a player by hitting it on the left or right of the vertical mid-line.

Body Mass Index (BMI)   A convenient way to express the ratio of height to weight and give a simple estimate of abnormal weight for height. BMI is weight (kilograms) divided by the height (metres) squared and should lie in the range 17–25.

Caffeine   A drug found in tea, coffee, chocolate and some carbonated beverages. Promotes fatty acid release, affects the cardiovascular system and is a diuretic.

Calorie   A very small, precisely defined unit of heat. One thousand calories are equivalent to one kilocalorie or kcal.

Carbohydrates   Molecules containing carbon, hydrogen and oxygen. They may be small simple units, often sweet, such as glucose, sucrose or larger units, often tasteless, such as starch. We cannot digest all carbohydrates and some are termed 'unavailable'; these include cellulose (dietary fibre). Carbohydrates provide energy for the body, about 4kcals per gram or 120kcals per ounce.

Cardiorespiratory Exercise   Exercise such as running, cycling, swimming, or any exercise utilising large muscle groups for an extended period of time; develops the ability of the blood, heart, lungs and other systems of the body to persist in work.

Chip Pass   When a player makes the ball rise off the ground by hitting the underside of the ball with the lace-section of the boot. This type of pass is easier if the ground is wet and muddy or if the ball is rolling towards the player.

Clockwork Player   A player who does only as he or she is told by the manager or coach and who does not make decisions for himself or herself.

Close On or Close Down   When a player reduces the space between himself or herself and the opponent.

Conditioned Game   A practice session or game containing specific rules; for example when a player is only allowed two touches of the ball at each encounter.

Cool-Down   A period of light exercise and stretching after vigorous activity.

Decision Time   The time taken to receive information through the senses and then to decide what to do in relation to that information.

Dehydration   Loss of body fluid with inadequate replacement. Liable to result from excessive sweating, diarrhoea or vomiting.

Dietary Deficiency   Inadequate intake of an essential nutrient which results in reduced body stores of the nutrient and eventually affects body function. Diagnosis of a deficiency requires biochemical tests.

Dislocation   A displacement of the bony surfaces at a joint so that the ends of the bone do not meet, or meet incorrectly. Refer immediately to a doctor.

Doping   The use of substances which artificially improve or augment an athlete's performance.

Double Cover   When a goalkeeper keeps part of the body behind the hands when gathering the ball.

End-line   The line at the end of a grid or group of grids used during practice.

Far-Post Cross   When crossing the ball from the wing, this cross is to the goal-post furthest from the winger.

Fats   Molecules containing carbon, hydrogen and oxygen. The small molecules are called fatty acids and dietary fats are a mixture of different fatty acids often held together by another molecule of glycerol and are then referred to simply as fat. Fats provide energy, 9kcals per gram or 270kcals per ounce.

Feint   A movement of the body which disguises a player's real intention; for example to pretend to go to the left but finally to go to the right.

Flexibility   A component of physical fitness or form of exercise which refers to the stretching of muscles.

Floating the Ball   At a throw-in, the thrower gives a lofted pass to the receiving player rather than a direct throw at his or her feet – this gives the receiving player time to move and make contact with the ball.

Free Kick   A direct or indirect kick awarded to one team when an opposing team player disregards the rules.

Glycogen   The form in which the mammalian body stores carbohydrate. It is mainly stored in the liver and muscles and constitutes a very mobile but limited store of energy for the body. It can be used without the presence of oxygen, i.e. anaerobically.

Haemoglobin   The oxygen-carrying component of red blood cells composed of an iron-based substance.

Interpass   A series of passes between two players.

Isokinetic   A form of resistance training where a machine provides resistance which allows for constant limb speed.

Isometric   A form of resistance training where no movement takes place.

Isotonic   A form of resistance training involving the lifting of free-standing objects, such as barbells.

Jockeying   This is a movement used when defending as a player retreats in front of an attacker. The player needs to be well-balanced, sideways on to the attacker and with the feet shoulder-width apart.

Joule   A very small and precise measure of the amount of work. The energy in food is related to the amount of work it can generate and therefore sometimes the energy value of food is expressed in joules. One thousand joules form one kilojoule or kJ. One kcal is equivalent to 4.2kJ.

Leaving the Line   When a goalkeeper leaves the vicinity of the goal-line under the crossbar in order to catch or punch a high ball, or to engage an oncoming attacking player.

Left Flank   The left-hand side of the pitch in relation to the direction of play.

Ligaments   Strong bands of fibrous tissue which bind bones together at a joint.

Lobbing the Ball   To pass the ball over an opponent.

Lofting the Ball   Passing through the air, rather than along the ground.

Long Pass   A pass made over distances of more than 20 metres.

Mental Imagery   The process of practising a skill in your mind rather than through physical practice.

Minerals   Inert substances some of which are essential to the body for its functioning. Calcium, magnesium, sodium, potassium, phosphorus, iron and zinc are some of these essential minerals.

Movement Time   The time taken to initiate and complete a game technique or skill.

Muscular Endurance   The ability to contract a muscle, or group of muscles, continuously over time.

Near-Post Cross   When crossing a ball from the wing, this cross is to the goal-post nearest to the winger.

Nutrients   Those parts of food which are used by the body to allow functioning of cells. Carbohydrates and fats are 'burned' to provide energy for cells to work – internally in order to make more tissue, for example, and externally to propel the body. Protein, vitamins and minerals are all used by the cells to function normally.

One-Bounce   A practice where only one bounce of the ball is allowed before the next player touches the ball.

One-Touch   When a player is allowed only one touch of the ball in order to pass or shoot.

Optimum Speed   The speed a player can cope with in relation to the ball; it is seldom full speed.

Osteoarthritis   The surfaces of bones at a joint are covered in cartilage which may become worn away, particularly in a joint which has been previously damaged. The joint may be painful, swollen and stiff.

Osteoporosis   A condition, mainly in women, in which the bones become increasingly thin and brittle – it is caused by reduced sex hormones and possibly low intake of calcium.

Overload   System in which training is progressively increased.

Power   The combination of strength and speed.

Pre-Planned Tactics and Strategies   Game plans which are based on the knowledge of the strengths and weaknesses of the opposing team and the strengths and weaknesses of your own team.

Progressive Muscle Relaxation (PMR)   A form of relaxation training which teaches the recognition of tension and relaxation through a series of muscle–tension exercises.

Proprioceptive Neuromuscular Facilitation (PNF)   A form of flexibility training which requires the muscle to be contracted before stretching.

Protein   That part of food which contains amino acids. It can be used for energy and provides 4kcals per gram or 120kcals per ounce.

Right Flank   The right-hand side of the pitch in relation to the direction of play.

Screening the Ball   When a player shields the ball from an opponent by placing his or her body between the opponent and the ball, stopping the opponent from making contact with the ball.

Short Pass   A pass made over a distance of up to 20 metres.

Side Preference   A goalkeeper continually uses one particular side of the body for diving or for going down at a player's feet.

Skinfold Thickness   The layer of body fat lying directly beneath the skin which can be measured using skinfold callipers. This layer of fat is related to total body fat which may be estimated from this method.

Sorbothane   A synthetic substance which absorbs energy well and is used as a 'shock-absorber' for inserts into shoes, mainly at the heel.

Spatial Awareness   A player's awareness of the space around him or her in relation to the proximity of colleagues and opponents.

Spinning Turn   A turn through 180 degrees with the foot on the ball.

Sports Anaemia   Probably not a true anaemia; the increase in plasma volume brought on by a serious training schedule dilutes the red cells reducing their concentration, the total number of red cells remaining the same.

Sprain   An injury to the ligaments around a joint which may produce pain, swelling and discolouration.

Step-Over   When a player passes his or her foot over the ball in order to deceive an opponent into thinking the ball will go to the left or right; after passing the foot over the ball the player accelerates away in the other direction.

Strength   The ability of the muscle to exert force.

Stress Fracture   A minute crack in a bone due to repeated overloading by an inappropriately rapid increase in training loads.

Tendon   White 'cords' which attach muscles to bones. They may become inflamed (tendonitis), partially torn, or completely broken (ruptured tendon).

Thread Pass   The movement of one player in advance of a colleague, in order to receive a pass.

Tonicity of Fluid   The concentration of particles in a solution compared to the concentration of particles in body fluids, especially blood. If the concentration in a solution is greater than blood it is termed hypertonic; if lower in concentration, hypotonic. Water will travel from a less concentrated solution to a more concentrated solution.

Variable Resistance Training   A form of resistance training which varies the loading to accommodate the mechanical efficiency of the body levers so that optimal tension is placed on the muscle throughout the whole range of movement.

Vitamins   Molecules which are found in food and are essential to cells for their efficient functioning. Some vitamins are associated and soluble in fat (vitamins A, D, E, K), others are soluble in water (vitamins B and C).

Volley   To kick the ball before it bounces.

Volley Touch   To return the ball to a colleague with one touch using the head, thigh, feet or another part of the body before the ball touches the ground.

Warm-Up   Light, mainly aerobic and flexibility exercises prior to vigorous activity.

Further Reading

*particularly recommended

Game Skills

Hughes, C., *Soccer Tactics and Skills* (BBC, 1980)*
Wade, A., *The FA Guide to Training and Coaching* (Heinemann, 1967)

Physical and Mental Fitness

Albinson, J. and Bull, S., *A Mental Game Plan* (Spodym, 49, Twickenham Road, Teddington, Middlesex, 1988)*
Alter, M., *The Science of Stretching* (Human Kinetics, 1988)
Fleck, S. and Kraemer, W. *Designing Resistance Training Programmes* (Human Kinetics, 1987)*
Fox, E., *Sports Physiology* (Saunders College, 1979)
Hazeldine, R., *Fitness for Sport* (The Crowood Press, 1985)*
Hemery, D., *The Pursuit of Sporting Excellence* (Collins Willow, 1986)
Lear, P. J., *Weight Training* (A & C Black, 1988)
National Coaching Foundation, *Physiology and Performance* (1986)
National Coaching Foundation, *The Coach at Work* (1986)
National Strength and Conditioning Association Journal
Nideffer, R.M., *The Athlete's Guide to Mental Training* (Human Kinetics, 1985)
Railo, W., *Willing to Win* (Springfield Books, 1986)
Syer, J. and Connolly, C., *Sporting Body, Sporting Mind* (Cambridge University Press, 1984)*
Terry, P., *The Winning Mind* (Thorsons, 1989)*

Nutrition

DHSS, *Recommended Amounts of Food Energy and Nutrients for Groups of People in the UK* (Report on Health and Social Subjects No. 15, 1979)
Eisenmann, P. and Johnson D., *Coaches' Guide to Nutrition and Weight Control* (Human Kinetics, 1982)
Haskell, W. *et al., Nutrition and Athletic Performance* (Bull Publishing, 1982)
Ministry of Agriculture, Fisheries and Food, *Manual of Nutrition* (HMSO, 1985)
Paul, A. and Southgate, D., *McCance and Widdowson's 'The Composition of Foods'* (HMSO, 1978)

Sports Injuries

Anderson, B., *Stretching* (Pelham, 1980)
Grisogono, V., *Sports Injuries: a Self-Help Guide* (John Murray, 1983)*
National Coaching Foundation, *Safety First for Coaches* (1986)
Read, M. and Wade P., *Sports and Medicine* (Butterworth, 1981)
St John Ambulance, *First Aid Manual* (Dorling Kindersley, 1982)

Useful Addresses

British Amateur Weight Lifters' Association, 3 Iffley Turn, Oxford OX4 4DY.

British Association of Sports Sciences, c/o National Coaching Foundation (*see* below)

Football Association, 16 Lancaster Gate, London W2 3LW.

Football League, Lytham St Annes, Lancashire, FY8 1JG.

National Coaching Foundation, 4 College Close, Beckett Park, Leeds LS6 3QH.

National Strength & Conditioning Association, P.O. Box 81410, Lincoln, Nebraska 68501, USA.

Professional Footballers' Association, 124 Corn Exchange Buildings, Hanging Ditch, Manchester M4 3BN.

Sports Council, 16 Upper Woburn Place, London WC1H 0QP.

St John Ambulance, Supplies Department, Priory House, St John's Gate, Clerkenwell, London EC1M 4DA.

Women's Football Association, 11 Portsea Mews, Portsea Place, London W2.

Index